Business Letters for Busy People

Edited by

National Press Publications

National Press Publications

A Division of Rockhurst University Continuing Education Center, Inc.

6901 West 63rd St. • P.O. Box 2949 • Shawnee Mission, KS 66201-1349

1-800-258-7246 • 1-913-432-7757

National Press Publications endorses nonsexist language. In an effort to make this handbook clear, consistent and easy to read, we have used "he" throughout the odd-numbered chapters and "she" throughout the even-numbered chapters. The copy is not intended to be sexist.

Business Letters for Busy People
Published by National Press Publications, Inc.
Copyright 2002 National Press Publications, Inc.
A Division of Rockhurst University Continuing Education Center, Inc.

Printed in the United States of America

18 17 16

ISBN #1-55852-300-6

About Rockhurst University Continuing Education Center, Inc.

Rockhurst University Continuing Education Center, Inc. is committed to providing lifelong learning opportunities through the integration of innovative education and training.

National Seminars Group, a division of Rockhurst University Continuing Education Center, Inc., has its finger on the pulse of America's business community. We've trained more than 2 million people in every imaginable occupation to be more productive and advance their careers. Along the way, we've learned a few things — what it takes to be successful ... how to build the skills to make it happen ... and how to translate learning into results. Millions of people from thousands of companies around the world turn to National Seminars for training solutions.

National Press Publications is our product and publishing division. We offer a complete line of the finest self-study and continuous-learning resources available anywhere. These products present our industry-acclaimed curriculum and training expertise in a concise, action-oriented format you can put to work right away. Packed with real-world strategies and hands-on techniques, these resources are guaranteed to help you meet the career and personal challenges you face every day.

Legend Symbol Guide

Checklists that will help you identify important issues for future application.

Table of Contents

How to Run the *Business Letters for Busy People* CD

Insert the CD into the CD drive. The program will start automatically after a few seconds, launching Adobe® Acrobat® Reader® and *Business Letters for Busy People*.

Users may receive the following message when launching Acrobat: "You cannot currently view Adobe PDF files from within your Web browser due to a configuration problem. Would you like Acrobat to fix the configuration?" Select Yes to continue.

Running the CD Manually

If your CD drive is set to AutoPlay, Acrobat Reader will launch *Business Letters* in a new window. If AutoPlay is disabled, double-click on My Computer, then double-click on your CD icon, which will say *Business Letters*. The program will launch Acrobat Reader and the book.

How to Navigate the CD

This CD features a navigation menu, located at the top and bottom of each page. Each of the following navigation methods has unique features to help you find information on the CD.

1. Table of Contents — You can get to any point in the book by clicking the listing in the table of contents or the corresponding page number.

2. Index — You can also use the index to find a specific item anywhere in the book. Click on a letter in the top navigation menu and you'll go to that part of the index. Then click on a page number to go to that page.

3. Search — The search function allows you to enter a key word and find it throughout the book. Click Search in the main navigation menu and enter your search word. Click Find and the program will highlight the first occurrence of the word. Click Find Again to move to the next occurrence. You can fine-tune your search using the Match Case, Match Whole Word and Find Backwards options in the search dialog box

4. Back — Click the Back button on the main navigation menu to retrace your path through each page you've visited in the book.

5. The page number in the navigation bar is bracketed by two arrows. Click on the right arrow to move to the next page. Click on the left arrow to move to the previous page.

Opening and Using Document Templates

Once you've located the letter you want, open the document template by clicking on the link in the right-hand margin. The program will open the letter with your Microsoft® word processor, then you can edit and personalize the letter as you wish.

Acrobat Reader runs *Business Letters* from the CD. You do not need Acrobat Reader installed on your hard drive. If you have another version of Acrobat Reader on your computer, you must close it before running the *Business Letters* CD.

You will encounter a warning dialog box when you open a document template each time you use *Business Letters*. Don't worry. There are no risks in using *Business Letters.* The purpose of this warning is to make you aware of the risks associated with using external files from unfamiliar sources. Click Open to launch the template. Check "Do not show this message again" to turn the warning off for the duration of your *Business Letters* session.

If you have questions, feedback or want more information, please contact us at *support@natsem.com.*

For additional information about using Acrobat Reader please go to Adobe's home page at *www.adobe.com.*

License Agreement
Users must accept the terms of the license agreement to use the CD.

*I*NTRODUCTION

Business Letters for Busy People is designed to be used, not just read. You not only get the easy-to-read impact of chapter-by-chapter "how to" information, but each section is also filled with checklists, ready-to-use letters and guidelines to help you do your job better, more effectively, more easily — right now! It's literally a user's manual for the business professional.

Business Letters for Busy People is packed with the most concrete information, useful techniques and practical tips possible in the smallest space. So you don't have to wade through endless pages of fluff searching for that elusive kernel of wisdom.

Business Letters for Busy People gives you concise, easy-to-use learning resources that get results. Check out the format and don't be surprised if you find yourself leafing through the pages for tidbits of fact and business trivia. The margins deliberately focus your attention, acting like a thumbnail index. And, each chapter is tabbed on the margins so you can turn right to the chapter you need to see. Read the chapters that are immediately important to you. Although there is a logic and order to the design of the book, you can read it in the order that best suits you. Each chapter stands alone.

We know you'll find this book helpful. Read it, copy it and act on its advice. Reading a good book awakens our minds, but too often never gets carried into action; we close the book unchanged. With this book, your reading becomes action — and action is the key to success.

Gary Weinberg
Vice President
National Press Publications

CHAPTER 1

Writing From Scratch

You are busy no matter what your position. Since you are busy, you want to use your time as effectively as possible. The business letter takes time but can be written more quickly if you follow a few basic principles. (If you're in a hurry, skip to Chapters 4–13 for samples of the kinds of letters you need to write.) This chapter assumes you have a little free time to brush up on business letter writing.

Keep in mind these three points when you write a letter:

1. Business letters serve one purpose.

2. Business letters are expensive.

3. Business letters serve as a record.

Business letters serve one purpose: They communicate information. Countless hours are spent, and too many letters are sent that say little or nothing. That's a waste of time for the sender and the receiver. Also, when the wages of the writer and the typist — along with the prorated cost of equipment and postage — are figured in, business letters are expensive. It is important that they be cost-effective. Why write a business letter? Because business letters serve as a record. Letters are long-lasting, tangible evidence of information you communicate to others.

In a study of 800 letters written by the top chief executive officers in the U.S., all 800 letters were found to be short, clear and personal.

By the time these people became CEOs, they had learned never to send out a letter that didn't reflect those three basic principles of good writing.

Four Considerations of a Business Letter

The four areas you must take into consideration for each business letter are listed below. If you do not consider each one of them, your letter will be ineffective.

1. Subject

2. Audience

3. Purpose

4. Style/Organization

Subject

Every piece of writing — from the business letter to the novel — revolves around a subject. Luckily, in the business world the subject is usually specific. Quite often it is supplied for you by someone else, such as a boss or colleague, or demanded by a situation such as hiring or congratulating an employee.

It's a fact: The more specific your subject, the easier it is to write your letter. For example, let's say that you need to request information about an order that did not arrive when it should have. If you are in charge of the account, writing the letter is easy. If you are not in charge of the account, it is harder for you to write the letter than it is for the person who knows all the particulars. Regardless of the situation, stick to one or two subjects in your letter. Including more than two subjects clouds your message. Write another letter if you have more than two subjects.

Audience

This area is tricky because you may not know your audience. If you do, you can tailor your letter to that audience. Many times, however, your audience is larger than you expect. Your letter may be addressed to Terry Smith but may be read by several other people in Terry's firm to receive the action you wish. If you are unsure of your audience, assume they are educated, reasonable people until you find out otherwise. Don't assume they have as much knowledge of the subject of your letter as you do, or you may overgeneralize or forget to include important details.

Purpose

Many letters are sent with a specific subject and audience in mind but are not clear in their purpose.

Know why you are sending the letter. Is the letter to inform? Is it to request information? Is it to offer congratulations? Condolences? Is it to get the recipient to act on a request? All of these are very different purposes. You have probably received a letter that, after reading it, left you confused because you didn't know exactly what it said. The purpose was not clear.

Style/Organization

The first three areas dictate the content, direction and emphasis of the letter.

1. Know WHAT you're writing about — SUBJECT.

2. Know WHO you're writing for — AUDIENCE.

3. Know WHY you're writing — PURPOSE.

Now you are ready to be concerned with HOW you are going to write the letter. The first three areas can be determined in a matter of minutes if you are familiar with the ideas that need to be communicated. The fourth area — style and organization — takes more time. (If you're pressed for time, refer to the sample letters in Chapters 4-13.)

Organization

Most of this book is devoted to the way different types of letters are organized. However, the basic organization for the body of a business letter follows.

Part 1 of Body	State your purpose.
Part 2 of Body	Explain what you want to happen or explain the information you have.
Part 3 of Body	Request a dated action, conclude or thank the reader for his response.

Notice that these are parts or sections rather than paragraphs. In some cases, particularly Part 2, the parts may consist of more than one paragraph. Let's take a look at each of these parts.

The "So What?" Test

When you have finished a draft of your letter, read each paragraph and ask yourself, "So what?" in the same way a new reader might. If you can't answer that from the paragraph, consider leaving it out.

"Brevity is the soul of wit."

— William Shakespeare

Part 1 of the Body

Get right to the point in the first sentence of the letter. When you read a novel, you expect to have background information before the story ever starts. When you read a business letter, you expect to be told immediately what will happen. Remember, your reader doesn't have any more time to wade through a long letter than you do.

This part is usually a short paragraph. Anything too long will cause the reader to lose patience.

Part 2 of the Body

This is the bread and butter of the letter. It explains the information you are giving, or it explains what you want the recipient to do. It doesn't need to be elaborate, but it does need to include all of the information the recipient needs.

If you have a lot of information, break it into short paragraphs, make a list or refer to an attachment. Underlining essential information is one way to highlight key points for your reader.

Your letter should be organized to help the recipient understand what to know or what to do.

Part 3 of the Body

This, like the first part, is usually a short paragraph. In writing classes, it's called the clincher — not a bad way to remember its function. Depending on the purpose of your letter, it will do one of three things.

1. **Conclude.** In an informational letter, this allows you to point out the most important item or draw all your key points into one statement.

2. **Request action.** In letters that require a response, such as collection letters, you define the action you want the recipient to take. In this part, you tell the reader what to do and when to do it. Being vague gets vague results. Be specific.

3. **Thank the reader.** In some letters, this part is simply a thank you for the recipient's attention, response or concern.

Tell 'em what you're going to say, say it, and tell 'em what you said.

- *State your purpose.*
- *Explain what you want to happen or explain the information you have.*
- *Request a dated action, conclude, thank the reader.*

In many ways, the method of writing a business letter is like the rule of thumb for giving a speech: Tell them what you're going to talk about. Talk about it. Then tell them what you talked about.

The following sample letter shows how each of the three parts work.

Capital Supplies
8995 Camden Rd. • Williamsburg, WI 63094

October 2, 20XX

Lance Smith, Director
Terrance Trucking
P.O. Box 4440
Houston, TX 34598-4440

Dear Mr. Smith:

Thank you for your conscientious service. All 15 of your last shipments have arrived undamaged. We have never contracted with a supplier with as fine a record as yours. We appreciate the extra effort it takes to ship our order intact and on time.

State Your Purpose

Ted McCracken and Bob Smiley have delivered these shipments to our loading dock supervisor. I have attached copies of logs for your review. Note that the unloading time is approximately half of that from other shippers for a similar load. Ted and Bob frequently help our crew unload the crates. This additional service always comes with an exchange of jokes. Our crew collects laughs to compete with your drivers!

Explain What You Want to Happen or Explain the Information You Have

Doing business with your organization is a pleasure. You save us money by eliminating shipping waste and time by providing efficient drivers. Please accept the enclosed certificates of merit to Terrance Trucking, Ted and Bob, with our appreciation. We are confident in referring our customers and vendors to Terrance Trucking for their shipping needs.

Request a Dated Action, Conclude, Thank the Reader

Sincerely,

Cala Reginald
CLR:mjk
Enc. (10)

Style is how you write the letter. Business letters used to be written in what might be called "businessese," a formal, stiff language. That is no longer true. The predominant style is matter-of-fact and conversational. Gone are such phrases as "the aforementioned" and "due to the fact that." Our high-tech, impersonal society requires business professionals to be more personable in their written communication in order to be more effective. The Seven "C's" of Style will help you become more effective.

The Seven "C's" of Style

1. **Conversational.** Write the way you speak. Get rid of stilted phrases. Why say "due to the fact that" when you can say "because"? Would you normally say "the aforementioned information"? Why not "the information" or, if you need to refer to a point, "the previous information"?

2. **Clarity.** The goal of clarity is that the reader understands precisely what you are saying. The language of your letter should be adapted to the recipient. This means that you write in a matter-of-fact, conversational tone. Use specific examples the reader can relate to. Don't assume that your reader understands the jargon of your trade. Remember, most letters will be read by people other than the recipient of the letter. These people may be unfamiliar with the technical language or jargon you use. Clarity also means organizing your letter so each paragraph deals with only one main idea and presenting your ideas in a logical order. Your letter should not be a collection of random ideas. It should be single-minded in its purpose.

3. **Concise.** A concise letter eliminates all unnecessary words. Why use four words, "in as much as," when you can use one word, "because"? This is not to say that you can't write long letters, but the longer the letter, the more ineffective it becomes. It is better to write a short letter with attachments than a long, detailed one. Short letters are read and remembered; long letters are skimmed and filed.

"Writing, when properly managed, is but a different name for conversation."

— Laurence Sterne

4. **Complete.** Make sure you have included all the information the reader needs to know. (Don't include details that are interesting but not relevant.) The biggest problem with leaving out information is that the reader has to make assumptions. For example, don't say, "When we last spoke about the situation," when you can say, "When we spoke on June 8 about hiring a new administrative assistant."

   Remember that the reader can't read your mind. The reader can only guess at what you left out.

5. **Concrete.** Use specific terms that cannot be misunderstood. Don't say, "The large order that we requested has not arrived." Say, "The order for 10,000 basins that we requested on May 3, 20XX, has not arrived as of June 20." Identify names and numbers.

   Write about what people can count or do. Include what people can see, touch, smell, taste or hear. In other words, make your language tangible. Make it concrete.

6. **Constructive.** Use words and phrases that set a positive tone. Constructive words are like smiling when you greet someone. They leave a good impression. Words such as "failure," "you neglected" and "error" tend to distance the recipient from the writer. Words such as "agreeable," "proud" and "success" help create a positive tone.

7. **Correct.** The last step in writing any business letter is to proofread it. You automatically check your image in a mirror before going out or meeting someone. The letter you send is your image on paper. If it is riddled with spelling, grammatical and typographical errors, it will detract from what you are trying to get across. The reaction will be, "He can't spell," or "She doesn't know how to type."

   If you have a secretary, don't assume your secretary knows how to spell or punctuate. Luckily, most do, but proof your own letters. Why? Because it is your name that is signed at the bottom of the page, not your secretary's. You will be the one who looks bad.

> *"Proper words in proper places make the true definition of style."*
>
> — Jonathan Swift

In a Nutshell

Writing a business letter need not be difficult as long as you remember that you are communicating with another business person just like yourself. If you incorporate Subject, Audience, Purpose and Style/Organization into your correspondence, you will be on the road to better business letter writing.

CHAPTER 2

Parts of a Business Letter

There are many parts to the business letter — some required, some optional. This chapter will review those parts and their order. The parts of the business letter follow:

1. Letterhead or Heading
2. Date
3. File Number (optional)
4. Confidential (optional)
5. Inside Address
6. Attention Line (optional)
7. Salutation (optional)
8. Subject Line (optional)
9. Body of the Letter
10. Complimentary Close (optional)
11. Signature
12. Added Information (optional)
13. Postscript (optional)
14. Mailing Instructions (optional)

Letterhead

Most business letters originating from a firm are written on the firm's letterhead. If you are writing a personal business letter or your firm does not use letterhead, then you need to include your firm's address in the heading (see Chapter 3 for the various formats).

Date

When you are using a heading instead of letterhead, place the date on the first line and the address on the subsequent lines as follows:

September 9, 20XX

359 Longview Road
Mt. Vernon, IL 65676

This should be the date the letter is written (see Chapter 3 for placement in the various formats). Be sure to write out the month and to include both the date and year for adequate reference.

> *The standard dateline in the U.S. is month/day/year: (March 15, 20XX).*
>
> *In Europe, however, the most widely used format is day/month/year: (15 March 20XX).*

File Number

On occasion, you may wish to include the file number of the project, case or order that the letter refers to. The file number should be physically separated from the date by two spaces and from the part that follows (Confidential or Inside Address) by two spaces.

Confidential

Use this word when the person to whom the letter is addressed is the only one who should read the letter. Physically separate the word from the rest of the letter by two lines. To assure confidentiality, include the word "Confidential" on the envelope.

Inside Address

This should include the name of the person you are writing to, the person's title (if available), the name of the firm and the firm's address.

Attention Line

This is used when you do not know the name of the person you are writing to and the letter is addressed to the firm. For example, the attention line may say, "Attention: Head of Accounting." It may also be used when you know the name of the person you are writing to but are unsure of the title. The attention line may say, "Attention: Customer Service," thus indicating to the person receiving the letter that the letter also needs to be routed to the customer service department. Another way of doing this is to use the attention line and send copies of the letter to the appropriate department.

Salutation

The salutation is used in all formats (see Chapter 3) except the Simplified Letter and the Memo. The following are salutations used in American business letters.

- Dear Sir

- Dear Madam (May be followed by title, such as Dear Madam Chairperson.)

- Gentlemen

- Ladies

- Dear Mr. Bryan

- Dear Ms. Gray

- Ladies and Gentlemen

- Dear Personnel Director (a gender-free title)

- To Whom It May Concern or TO WHOM IT MAY CONCERN (Use this form as a last resort.)

Caution: You must determine the appropriate choice, given your reader and the situation. If you are uncertain about your reader's gender, avoid assuming gender in the salutation. Use your reader's name whenever you know it. Researchers discovered that people are more likely to read a letter with their names in the salutation.

People don't usually get upset if you don't address them with the proper salutation, but they notice and appreciate it when you do.

2

One of the problems you may run into is writing to a person with a name that is not gender specific; for example, the name Terry. The simplest solution in the salutation is to say, "Dear Terry Lucas." If you are addressing a group of people in general, such as the shipping department, do not assume they are all male. The old "Gentlemen" is not acceptable. "Shipping Agents" is preferred. The way around having to use a salutation when you are unsure of whom you are writing is to use the Simplified Letter (see Chapter 3).

Subject Line

The subject line is most commonly used in the Simplified Letter. It announces the subject of the letter and provides a summary of your intent.

Body of the Letter

This is where you make requests, provide information or reasons, or reply to someone. It is the main part of the business letter (see Chapter 3 for the various body formats).

Complimentary Close

This varies in formality and is found in all business letters with the exception of the Simplified Letter and the Memo (see Chapter 3 for its placement). The following complimentary closes are in order of decreasing formality:

- Very truly yours
- Respectfully
- Sincerely yours
- Cordially
- Sincerely

The most appropriate, in general situations, is the last.

Unless you're aiming for the Nobel prize, you shouldn't worry about your writing talent. Writing good business documents is a craft, not an art. It requires skill, not talent, and you can learn skills.

Signature

There should be four lines between the complimentary close (or the body in the Simplified Letter) and your typed name so there is room for your signature.

Additional Information

If needed, this consists of the sender's initials in capital letters followed by a colon, followed by the typist's initials in small letters. You may also find the abbreviations "Enc." for enclosure and "cc:" or "xc:" for copies sent, followed by names of persons receiving the copies.

Postscript

The "P.S." highlights additional information that might have been placed in the letter but for some reason was not. Often used in sales, promotional or personal letters, the postscript can emphasize a request for action or consideration. It is often the first thing the recipient reads. Use it to entice or motivate your reader. Postscripts are especially effective in sales or form letters.

Mailing Instructions

Use these to give the reader deadlines or pertinent information on mailing a reply.

As you look through the major formats in Chapter 3, it's obvious that many of the parts listed above are not necessarily used in routine business correspondence. However, it helps to be aware of all of them in case you need to use any of them.

CHAPTER 3

Format of a Business Letter

Business letter formats have changed over the years. If you went to school prior to the 1970s, you probably learned one basic form of business letter now called the Modified Semi-Block. It was the bane of every beginning typist because of its strict rules concerning spacing. Luckily, the movement in business has been to simplify and provide choices. Now you have a choice of six different forms, some extremely simple, others more complex. This chapter will review the various forms. The six forms of business letters most commonly used are:

- Block
- Modified Block
- Modified Semi-Block

- Simplified
- Hanging Indented
- Memo

It is likely that your organization may prefer one form over another. In the following explanations, the assumption is that you will be using letterhead stationery. If you are writing a personal business letter without letterhead, place your address one line above or below the date as in the following examples:

August 3, 20XX

2578 Tarrymore Lane
Chicago, IL 66557-1234

    or 2578 Tarrymore Lane
Chicago, IL 66557-1234

August 3, 20XX

3

The state in the sender's address and the inside address may be written out in a formal letter or abbreviated with the two-letter postal service code in an informal letter. As the postal service's recommendation to use the new format for envelope addresses gains momentum, we will see another change in the business letter: The inside address may match the envelope address to eliminate the need for two separate databases for address styles. Both can look like this:

2578 TARRYMORE LANE
CHICAGO IL 66557-1234

All letters are capitalized, and no line punctuation is used, which allows the electronic scanners to sort the mail more quickly. The nine-digit ZIP code is also gaining popularity to process and deliver mail more quickly.

Block

The Block format is by far the simplest. Every part of the letter starts at the left margin, with spaces between each part. It has a professional look to it. The order for the parts of the letter are date, file number, inside address, attention line, salutation, subject line, body, complimentary close, signature, typed name and additional information.

Italics Unlimited 231 W. 40th Street • Camden, NJ 08618 • (623) 555-2678	*Letterhead*
August 10, 20XX	*Date (2-3 spaces)*
XXX	*File Number*
Terry Lancaster Capital Supply 657 Minden Ct. Des Moines, Iowa 54687	*Inside Address* *(2-3 spaces)*
Attention: President of Capital Supply	*Attention Line* *(2-3 spaces)*
Dear Mr. Lancaster:	*Salutation* *(2-3 spaces)*
Subject: XXXXXXXX	*Subject Line*
XXXXXXXXXXXXXXXXXXXXXXXXXXXXXXXXXXXXXX XXXXXXXXXXXX	*Body* *(2 spaces between* *paragraphs)*
XXXXXXXXXXXXXXXXXXXXXXXXXXXXXXXXXXXXXX XXXXXXXXXX	
Sincerely,	*Complimentary* *Close (4 spaces for* *signature)*
Signature	*Signature*
Joan McAllister	*Typed Name* *(2-3 spaces)*
JFM:eer	
P.S. XXXXXXXXX	*Additional* *Information* *Postscript*
XXXXXXXXX	*Mailing Instructions*

3

Modified Block

Like the Block, the Modified Block has the advantage of separating paragraphs so that each one stands out. The spacing between sections remains the same as in the Block. The date, signature and closing are placed to the right, thus allowing them to stand out. The complimentary close and the signature are aligned and placed near the center of the letter, two spaces below the last paragraph.

Italics Unlimited
231 W. 40th Street • Camden, NJ 08618 • (623) 555-2678

Letterhead

August 10, 20XX

Date (right of center)

Terry Lancaster
Capital Supply
657 Minden Ct.
Des Moines, Iowa 54687

Inside Address
(left margin)

Dear Mr. Lancaster:

Salutation (2-3 spaces)

XXXXXXXXXXXXXXXXXXXXXXXXXXXXXXXXXXXXXXXX
XXXXXXXXXXXXXXXXXXXXXXXXXXXXXXXXXXXXXXXX
XXXXXXXXXXXXXXXXX

Body
(left margin with 2 spaces between paragraphs)

XXXXXXXXXXXXXXXXXXXXXXXXXXXXXXXXXXXXXXXX
XXXXXXXXXXXXXXXXXXXXXXXXXXXXXXXXXXXXXXXX
XXXXXXXXXXXX

Sincerely,

Signature

Joan McAllister

Complimentary Close (right of center)
Signature (right of center)
Typed Name
Additional Information (left margin)

JFM:eer

Modified Semi-Block

3

You will recognize the Modified Semi-Block as the format most commonly taught as "the business letter." It is the same as the Modified Block except that the paragraphs are indented five spaces. All spacing remains the same.

<table>
<tr><td align="center">**Italics Unlimited**
231 W. 40th Street • Camden, NJ 08618 • (623) 555-2678</td><td>*Letterhead*</td></tr>
<tr><td align="right">August 10, 20XX</td><td>*Date (right of center)*</td></tr>
<tr><td>Terry Lancaster
Capital Supply
657 Minden Ct.
Des Moines, Iowa 54687</td><td>*Inside Address*
(left margin)</td></tr>
<tr><td>Dear Mr. Lancaster:</td><td>*Salutation*</td></tr>
<tr><td>   XXXXXXXXXXXXXXXXXXXXXXXXXXXXXXXXX
XXXXXXXXXXXXXXXXXXXXXXXXXXXXXXXXX
XXXXXXXXXXXXXX

    XXXXXXXXXXXXXXXXXXXXXXXXXXXXXXXXX
XXXXXXXXXXXXXXXXXXXXXXXXXXXXXXXXX
XXXXXXXXXXX</td><td>*Body*
(indent paragraphs 5
spaces and separate
paragraphs with 2
spaces)</td></tr>
<tr><td align="right">Sincerely,</td><td>*Complimentary Close*
(right of center)</td></tr>
<tr><td align="right">*Signature*</td><td>*Signature*
(right of center)</td></tr>
<tr><td align="right">Joan McAllister</td><td>*Typed Name*
(right of center)</td></tr>
<tr><td>JFM:eer</td><td>*Additional Information*
(left margin)</td></tr>
</table>

3

Simplified

This is useful when you do not know the title of the person you are writing to or when you are writing to a company, government agency or organization. It eliminates the courtesy titles (Mr., Mrs., Ms., Dr.), the salutations and the complimentary close. The focus of the letter is on the body and what is to be said. The spacing is the same as the Block format.

Italics Unlimited 231 W. 40th Street • Camden, NJ 08618 • (623) 555-2678	*Letterhead*
August 10, 20XX	*Date*
Terry Lancaster Capital Supply 657 Minden Ct. Des Moines, Iowa 54687	*Inside Address*
SUBJECT: PRINTING SUPPLIES	*Subject of Letter (highlight this summary line with capitalization, bold face or underlining)*
XXXXXXXXXXXXXXXXXXXXXXXXXXXXXXXXXXX XXXXXXXXXXXXXXXXXXXXXXXXXXXXXXXXXXX XXXXXXXXXXXXXXXXX	
XXXXXXXXXXXXXXXXXXXXXXXXXXXXXXXXXX XXXXXXXXXXXXXXXXXXXXXXXXXXXXXXXXXX XXXXXXXXXXXXX	*Body (2 spaces between paragraphs)*
Signature	*Signature*
Joan McAllister	*Typed Name Additional Information*
JFM:eer	

20

Hanging Indented

On occasion you will see this form but, for all practical purposes, it is seldom used. Its main advantage is that it calls attention to the body and each of the paragraphs. Spacing between the lines and sections is the same as in previous examples.

Italics Unlimited 231 W. 40th Street • Camden, NJ 08618 • (623) 555-2678	*Letterhead*
August 10, 20XX	*Date (right of center)*
Terry Lancaster Capital Supply 657 Minden Ct. Des Moines, Iowa 54687	*Inside Address (2-3 spaces)*
Dear Mr. Lancaster:	*Salutation*
XXXXXXXXXXXXXXXXXXXXXXXXXXXXXXXXXXX XXXXXXXXXXXXXXXXXXXXXXXXXXXXXXXXX XXXXXX XXXXXXXXXXXXXXXXXXXXXXXXXXXXXXXXXXX XXXXXXXXXXXXXXXXXXXXXXXXXXXXXX	*Body (indent second and subsequent lines in each paragraph)*
Sincerely,	*Complimentary Close (right of center)*
Signature	*Signature (right of center)*
Joan McAllister	*Typed Name (right of center)*
JFM:eer	*Additional Information (left margin)*

3

Memo

A sixth form of letter is the Memo. Though used primarily as an interoffice communication, it is occasionally used as a business letter format. The top of the Memo indicates the date, the name(s) of the recipient(s), the name(s) of the sender(s) and the subject. The abbreviation "RE" is sometimes used instead of "Subject." This information is placed at the left margin. The body of the Memo is in Block form. A signature and additional information are optional. The signature is often placed near the center with the additional information at the left margin.

MEMORANDUM	*Memo Information* *(2-3 spaces)*
Date: August 10, 20XX To: Terry Lancaster From: Joan McAllister Subject: Printing Supplies	
XXXXXXXXXXXXXXXXXXXXXXXXXXXXXXXXXXX XXXX XXXXXXXXXXXXXXXXXXXXXXXXXXXXXXXXXXX XXXXXXXXXXXXXXXXXXXXXXXXXXXXX XXXXXXXXXXXXXXXXXXXXXXXXXXXXXXXXX XXXXXXXXXXXXXXXXXXXXXXXXXXXXXXXXXXX XXXXXXXXXX	*Body* *(single-spaced lines, 2 spaces between paragraphs)*
Signature Joan McAllister	*Signature (2-3 spaces)* *Typed Name*
JFM:eer cc: Ted Kapstein, Marsha Little	*Additional Information (left margin)*

*C*HAPTER 4

Collection Letters

This chapter has sample collection letters you may have to write. The types of collection letters included are:

- Notification
- Reminder
- Inquiry
- Urgency
- Final Notice/Ultimatum
- Insufficient Funds
- Thank You for Payment
- Lost Payment/Apology

In this section, at the side of the page, you will find a brief explanation of each part of the letter. The first letter identifies each section of the letter. Subsequent letters identify only changes to the basic format.

> *"Creditors have better memories than debtors."*
>
> — Ben Franklin

4

Step-by-Step Guide

The purpose of the collection letter is to get the customer to pay an overdue bill.

Step 1: Check the spelling of the recipient's name. Use a gender-specific courtesy title only if you are certain of the recipient's gender. There is nothing more embarrassing or irritating than getting a collection letter, except getting one that is addressed improperly.

Step 2: The first part of the letter should state the concern and the situation (date purchased, amount owed and date due).

Step 3: The next part of the letter should indicate the deadline for paying the bill and any penalties that may result. You may also wish to indicate your company's policy concerning late payments, grace periods, penalties or alternative payment plans.

Step 4: The third part of the letter should indicate the consequences of not paying the bill. Initially, these may be penalties but, as the bill becomes more delinquent, it may include warnings of ruined credit ratings or involvement of a collection agency.

Step 5: The final part of the letter should encourage the recipient to send full payment or contact you to arrange a payment schedule. End with goodwill and a positive attitude that this situation will be resolved satisfactorily.

Note: At the end of this chapter is a checklist to use when you write collection letters.

Notification

This letter is to notify the recipient that the bill is overdue.

Western Wear 2212 Boot Hill Rd. • Cheyenne, WY 82001	*Letterhead*
July 5, 20XX	*Date (2-3 spaces)*
Ted Wilson 515 Ramey Ct. Laramie, WY 82063	*Inside Address* *(2-3 spaces)*
Dear Mr. Wilson:	*Salutation*
Thank you for shopping with us. You are a valued customer. We appreciate your business and know that you want to keep your account current with us.	*State the Concern*
On May 15, 20XX, you purchased merchandise worth $319.04 from our store in Laramie. Your payment of $100 is now overdue.	*State the Situation*
In the credit agreement you signed, you agreed to pay off your bill in three payments. The first payment of $100 was due June 15, 20XX. Please send this amount now.	*Indicate Deadline*
Failure to pay on time may affect your ability to charge merchandise at our store. Thank you for your prompt attention.	*Indicate Consequences*
You may call me at 800-555-9875 if you have any questions or concerns. Your continued patronage is important to us.	*Indicate Contact* *Indicate Goodwill*
Sincerely,	*Complimentary Close*
Signature	*Signature*
Mary West Credit Manager	*Typed Name*
MJW:cjl	*Additional Information*

4

4

Reminder

This letter reminds the reader that the bill is overdue and the payment still hasn't been received. Be careful to focus on observable behaviors and to avoid assumptions. Saying, "We have not received payment," is an observable behavior. Saying, "You have not sent payment," is an assumption. Stay positive.

Western Wear
2212 Boot Hill Rd. • Cheyenne, WY 82001

August 5, 20XX

Ted Wilson
515 Ramey Ct.
Laramie, WY 82063

Dear Mr. Wilson:

We have not yet received your payments. This is to remind you that both your first and second payments of $100 are now overdue. This $200 plus the balance of $119.04 is due on August 15.

Remind Recipient of the Situation

In the credit agreement you signed, you agreed to pay off your bill in three payments. The first payment of $100 was due June 15, 20XX, the second payment of $100 was due July 15, 20XX, and the final payment of $119.04 is due August 15, 20XX. Please send the full amount in 10 days.

Request Payment and Indicate Deadline

Failure to pay on time will affect your ability to charge merchandise at our store. If you want to discuss your account, call me at 800-555-9875. Perhaps we can arrange a more comfortable payment plan.

Indicate Consequences, Alternative and Contact

Thank you for your immediate attention.

Indicate Goodwill

Sincerely,

Signature

Mary West
Credit Manager

4

Inquiry

This letter inquires why the bill isn't being paid. It assumes that the bill is overdue. It's a good idea to follow this letter with a personal phone call inquiring about the payment delay. Often an alternative plan can be arranged to suit the recipient's current budget constraints. If another agreement is reached, send a copy of the new payment plan to the recipient. Continue to follow up letters with phone calls to maintain open communication. Keep a log of all calls.

Western Wear
2212 Boot Hill Rd. • Cheyenne, WY 82001

September 5, 20XX

Ted Wilson
515 Ramey Ct.
Laramie, WY 82063

Dear Mr. Wilson:

Is there some reason you have not paid your bill of $319.04? *Inquire*

In the credit agreement you signed, you agreed to pay off *Indicate Deadline*
your bill in three payments. Your total bill is now overdue.
Please send $319.04 within 10 days. If you have any
questions or concerns regarding this bill, please contact me *Indicate Contact*
at 800-555-9875 by September 10.

Failure to send the full amount by September 15 may mean *Indicate Consequences*
that your bill is turned over to a collection agency. Your
prompt attention is urgent to protect your credit.

Sincerely,

Signature

Mary West
Credit Manager

MJW:cjl

Urgency

This letter stresses the urgency of the need for the customer to take some kind of action on the bill. It is a continuing progress report on the recipient's account. If an alternative payment plan has been reached previously, indicate the details of the agreement and the telephone contact dates to keep an accurate record of communications.

Western Wear
2212 Boot Hill Rd. • Cheyenne, WY 82001

November 5, 20XX

Ted Wilson
515 Ramey Ct.
Laramie, WY 82063

Dear Mr. Wilson:

Your bill of $319.04 is now overdue 60 days. Send $319.04 within 10 days. If you cannot send the total, please call me at 800-555-9875.

State the Situation
Indicate Grace Period (indicate alternative, if agreed)

Failure to respond may mean that your bill is turned over to a collection agency. Thank you for your prompt attention.

Indicate Probable Consequences

Sincerely,

Signature

Mary West
Credit Manager

MJW:cjl

Final Notice/Ultimatum

This letter is the final notice the customer receives. It gives the customer an ultimatum: If you do not respond, this will happen. After this letter, there are no more chances.

4

Western Wear
2212 Boot Hill Rd. • Cheyenne, WY 82001

December 1, 20XX

Ted Wilson
515 Ramey Ct.
Laramie, WY 82063

Dear Mr. Wilson:

Your bill of $319.04 is now 90 days overdue.   *State the Situation*

The total amount is due now.   *Indicate Deadline*

If your payment in full is not received by December 10, your   *Indicate Consequences*
file will be turned over to a collection agency.

Sincerely,

Signature

Mary West
Credit Manager

MJW:cjl

Insufficient Funds

Sometimes a good customer sends a "bad" check.

4

Zenith Building Supplies
678 Central Parkway
Durham, NC 27715

August 13, 20XX

Tim Blackwell, President
Blackwell Builders
98 Diego Dr.
Durham, NC 27713

Dear Mr. Blackwell:

Thank you for your July 28 payment, check #1429 for $200. Unfortunately, it was returned by your bank because of insufficient funds.

I'm returning the check to you for your review. Please send a payment this week after you reconcile this matter with your bank. If we receive your payment by August 31, you will avoid accruing additional interest charges on your outstanding balance with us.

Your continued patronage is important to us. We appreciate your good payment record in the past year. We know that you, too, will be happy when this situation is resolved. If I can help, just call me at 800-555-1234.

Sincerely,

Signature

Jackie Quentin

Enc.

	Sender's Address
	Thank You
	State Problem
	Action Plan
	Goodwill

Thank You for Payment

A collection letter that is often neglected is the thank-you note. It can provide a reminder of both the account status and the customer's importance.

Word Trade, Inc.
5698 Adie Road • St. Ann, MO 63074

April 19, 20XX

Vern Mueller
13245 Greenwood Lane
Overland Park, KS 66213

Dear Mr. Mueller:

Thank you for your payment of $563.89. Your current balance is $3,000 — your credit limit. A payment of $500 is due May 1.

Thank You
Caution/Reminder

We appreciate your attention to your account status with us. Your patronage is important to our company.

Appreciation

If we can assist you, please contact us at 800-555-9000.

Contact Information

Sincerely,

Signature

Anita Collins
Account Executive

AC:etr

Lost Payment/Apology

Sometimes a bill adjustment and an apology are necessary.

Deem's Department Store
2030 Aquamarine Road
Silver Spring, MD 20904

August 4, 20XX

Mrs. Franklin
5930 E. 46th St.
Colesville, MD 20901

Dear Mrs. Franklin:

Your patience has been bountiful. When we last spoke on Friday, I had not yet located your payment. I have credited $45.89 to your account today.

Acknowledgment
Adjustment

Our policy states that one percent interest (APR) is accrued on the last workday of the month on any account balance. However, we are withdrawing this policy for you for August 1 through October 31, during which time your account will reflect a zero-interest adjustment.

Policy

Adjustment

We found your check (#984, dated June 20, 20XX) on our mailroom floor this morning. The envelope was torn away and the check was crumpled. We are still speculating about how it disappeared.

Reason

To offset any inconvenience the interim bills have caused you, we are enclosing a 20 percent discount coupon for your next order. Just attach the coupon to your order and I'll personally assist you.

Benefit

Thank you for your patience, Mrs. Franklin. Please accept our warmest apology.

Thank You
Apology

Sincerely,

Signature

Sybil Paxton
Customer Service Manager

SP:smm

Checklist

- Did you verify the name of the recipient?
- Was the tone of the letter firm but understanding?
- Did you state the amount owed?
- Did you state when the bill was originally due?
- Did you state the penalties, if any?
- Did you suggest an alternative payment plan?
- Did you state the grace period, if any?
- Did you state the new deadline?
- Did you summarize telephone contacts?
- Did you indicate the consequences of not paying the bill?

4

CHAPTER 5

Sales and Promotional Letters

Actually, all letters are sales letters in business. You are selling a service or product as well as your image as a business. These letters intend to initiate or close a sale. The broad categories follow:

- Request for Appointment
- Prospective Lead
- Sales Letters to Clients
- Letter of Introduction
- Follow-Up on Letter Sent
- Delinquent Reply
- Extremely Delinquent Reply
- Requesting Customer's Assistance
- Sales Follow-Up
- Confirming Sales Order
- Reminder That a Sale Is About to End
- Announcing a Sales Campaign, Promotion or Incentive Program
- Announcing a Sales Campaign to Preferred Customers
- Announcing New Products to a Select Group of Customers

- Announcing a Price Increase
- Transmittal Letters

At the side of the page, you will find a brief explanation of each part of the letter. The first letter identifies each section of the letter. Subsequent letters identify only changes to the basic format.

Step-by-Step Guide

Sales and promotional letters are used by salespeople to set up or confirm appointments, announce sales promotions, congratulate salespeople on their successes and introduce new salespeople to their clients. The letter itself is a sales tool. These letters are often more creative in content and composition than other kinds of letters.

Step 1: The first part of the letter states your purpose. Depending on the reason for writing the letter, this may vary from requesting an appointment to introducing a new salesperson. Your purpose is to stimulate the reader's interest. Identify the benefit to your recipient.

Step 2: The second part of the letter gives details or background information. This is the persuasive part of the letter. If you are making a request, then this part would give the reason for the request. For example, in a request for an appointment, the second part would set up the time for the appointment, provide the telephone number where you can be reached and state the location of the appointment. If you are introducing a new salesperson, this part would give his background.

Step 3: The last part of the letter acts as a statement of desired action and as a summary reminding the recipient of the letter's general nature. In many sales and promotional letters, this is a thank you; in others, it is a restatement of what has been said previously. It may also be used to summarize the details of an appointment. Many sales letters include a handwritten postscript to emphasize urgency or a benefit.

Note: At the end of this chapter is a checklist to use when you write a sales and promotional letter.

Request for Appointment

This letter is used by the salesperson to set up appointments and to announce his schedule. Include an added service or an "extra effort" to encourage the recipient to see you later. It is an introductory letter and should be followed up with another letter or phone call.

5

Carrington's 38 E. 91st St. • Chicago, IL 60614	*Letterhead*
January 25, 20XX	*Date*
Linda Montgomery, Manager A-1 Cleaners 2903 Burresh St. Lincoln, NE 68506	*Inside Address*
Dear Ms. Montgomery:	*Salutation*
I will be in Lincoln on February 3 and would like to meet with you at your office to discuss cleaning supplies you may need in the second half of the year.	*Request for Appointment*
I have enclosed our latest catalog. Please note the items in yellow highlight. They are special values or new products that A-1 Cleaners will want to take advantage of now.	*Added Service* *Benefit*
I will contact you later this week to schedule an appointment. If you need to get in touch with me, call me at 800-555-9047. I look forward to talking with you. Thank you for your continued business.	*Confirmation* *Contact Information* *Thank You*
Sincerely yours,	*Complimentary Close*
Signature	*Signature*
Douglas James Sales Representative	*Typed Name* *Title*
DNJ:llr Enc.	*Additional Information*
P.S. See page 68 of our catalog for a great value on our most-ordered product choice!	*Postscript*

Prospective Lead

This letter is a follow-up from a lead given to the salesperson. It introduces the salesperson to the prospective lead.

Tom's Sport Supply
665 Spinning Wheel Ct. • Bilmont, UT 84106

December 4, 20XX

Terrance O'Toole
Golfers Teed Off
870 C. Street
Walla Walla, WA 98661

Dear Mr. O'Toole:

You and your firm have been recommended by Cal Gonzonles of Fore, Inc. Cal indicated that you may be interested in the line of products that we have, particularly our new Golflite line. I have enclosed our latest catalog.

I will be in the Walla Walla area the week of December 16. I would like to meet with you to discuss how our Golflite line can help your business. I will contact you within the next 10 days to schedule an appointment. In the meantime, if you have any questions, call me at 800-555-1125. I look forward to meeting you.

Sincerely yours,

Signature

Chip Ashcroft
Sales Representative

CNA:pam
Enc.

Purpose

Reference
Added Service

Request for
Appointment

Contact Information

Sales Letter to Client

A sales letter is used to introduce the contact and generate interest.

WAVERLEY HOTEL
360 South Dearborn • Chicago, IL 60604

August 15, 20XX

Fred E. Sherman, Secretary
The Paramount Institute
P.O. Box 323
Orlando, FL 32822

Dear Mr. Sherman:

Just a note to introduce myself and to let you know of the Waverley Hotel's interest in the 20XX meeting plans of the Paramount Institute.

Reason for Letter

The Waverley Hotel contains 674 newly redecorated guest rooms; this includes 12 double room suites. The hotel is located in the heart of Chicago, only 30 minutes from Midway airport. Our three four-star restaurants offer our guests variety in menu selection and atmosphere. Our 36,000 square feet of meeting and banquet space include the city's largest ballroom and the largest on-site exhibition hall. I have enclosed a complete schedule of our function space dimensions and capacities.

Details

Enclosure

Please stop by and see us if you are in our area — we would like the opportunity to show off our hotel. In the meantime, however, I will call your office next week to answer any questions you may have on the Waverley's facilities and to discuss how we may be of service to the Paramount Institute.

States Follow-up Plans

Contact Information

Sincerely,

Signature

Carol Brawn
Director, Convention Services

JS:drb

Enc.

Sales Letter to Current Client

This letter asks an existing client for more business.

5

GERSON ACCOUNTING SERVICES P.O. Box 514 San Francisco, CA 94133	*Sender's Address*
September 10, 20XX	
John L. Hoffman United Services Bank P.O. Box 8976 San Francisco, CA 94133	
Dear Mr. Hoffman:	
This afternoon I spoke with Don Smith at the United Services Bank in Berkeley. During our conversation, Don mentioned that the bank uses a local CPA firm to maintain its book depreciation records.	*Statement of the Situation*
Since we prepare the tax return for United Services Bank, it would seem to make sense for us to maintain both systems. We would incur some set-up cost; however, this would be recouped over a relatively short period through efficiencies in running both depreciation systems through one software package.	*Reason* *Benefit*
If you are interested in this idea, I will put together an estimate of the set-up cost for you. For your information, since the bank's book depreciation system is in very good shape, I would anticipate our set-up time on this account to be less than what we have encountered in setting up other clients.	*Service* *Benefit*
Sincerely,	
Signature	
Steve Brooks Vice President	
JFS: dkf	

Letter of Introduction

This letter is used to introduce one person to another — such as a new salesperson to an established client. If you address the recipient by first name, you can do likewise with the person being introduced. If a courtesy title and a last name are more appropriate, be consistent with all the names that are mentioned in the salutation, body and closing signature.

5

Sea Lanes

8945 N. Shore Dr. • Boston, MA 01611 • 1-800-555-3456

November 22, 20XX

Carl N. White
Lobster Trappers Ltd.
Box 65
Kepaquadick Cove, ME 04103

Dear Carl:

I am happy to introduce our new sales representative, Terry King, to you. Terry will be in charge of servicing your account. | *Introduction*
Reason

Terry is a graduate of the University of Maine and holds a degree in Sales and Marketing. For the last five years he has worked as a salesman for Boston Fisheries and Equipment. We are proud to have him on our staff and are sure he will be able to give you the kind of service you have come to expect from Sea Lanes. | *Background Information*

Support

Please call us if there is anything we can do for you. Terry will be contacting you within the next two weeks to personally introduce himself, discuss his monthly schedule and answer any questions you might have. Ask Terry about his family's secret recipe for lobster! | *Request*

Contact Information

Personal Note

Sincerely yours,

Signature

T.K. (Tip) Walton
Director of Sales

TKW:joi

Follow-Up on Letter Sent

This letter asks the customer if he has received a letter.

Three W's
Box 231 • Medford, MO 64506

December 1, 20XX

Richard Patterson
789 Winterwood Lane
St. Joseph, MO 64503

Dear Mr. Patterson:

On November 10, I sent you a letter describing our newest product. Did you receive the letter? | *Reference*

I will be happy to answer any questions you may have and explain the unique features of Vu-More and its benefits to you. | *Purpose*

You are a valued customer. If there is any way that I can help you in making a decision, please call me at 800-555-1309. | *Compliment*
Assistance Offer and
Contact Information

Sincerely,

Signature

Kay Lynne Overmeyer
Sales Director

KLO:pst

Delinquent Reply

This letter is used to remind a customer who has not responded to a recent letter.

Lakeland Insurance
7779 23rd St. E. • Camden, NJ 08610

October 2, 20XX

Barry Wu
Wu's Gardens
558 Magnolia
Garden City, NJ 08638

Dear Mr. Wu:

Just a reminder: I recently sent you a computer printout of a proposal of health insurance for your employees.   *Reminder*

I have attached another printout for your convenience and hope that you will take the time to review it. As you can see,   *Review*
we offer a competitive package. Plans A and B are especially   *Emphasis*
responsive to your needs.

I will call you next Friday after you have had time to review   *Assistance Offer*
the proposal. I am eager to do business with you. In the
meantime, if you have any questions or concerns, I can be   *Contact Information*
reached at 308-555-9847.

Sincerely,

Signature

Terry Laforge
Sales Manager

TML:wie
Enc.

Extremely Delinquent Reply

This letter is used when a customer has not responded after a long period of time.

Cattleman's
3567 Hereford Lane • Tulsa, OK 73072

July 15, 20XX

J.M. Chesterman
900 Oilman Highway
Tinderbox, CO 80215

Dear Mr. Chesterman:

Yesterday I was going through our files and realized that we had neglected to contact you concerning our proposal to replace your cattle feeders.

Statement of the Situation

I realize that four months have passed since I sent you the information, so I have attached our original proposal. I hope you will take time to look it over. We feel our prices are very competitive and the quality and durability of our feeders will actually save you money in the long term.

Reference

Benefits

I will call you next Monday after you have had time to review the proposal. I am looking forward to doing business with you. If you have any questions or concerns, I can be reached at 308-555-9847.

Contact Information

Sincerely,

Signature

Theodore "Tex" Miller
President

TJM:ssm
Enc.

P.S. You can save $535 on a feeder this year!

Postscript

Requesting Customer's Assistance

This letter is used as a foot in the door and to request that a potential customer help the salesperson.

Martin Medical
3445 Medford Ave. • Charleston, SC 29624

March 17, 20XX

Terrance Reilly
Box 557
Camden Creek, SC 29625

Dear Mr. Reilly:

I would like your help in solving a problem that people in businesses such as yours have.

Assistance Request

Each year, businesses that sell medical supplies are faced with hundreds of new products. We would like your assistance in answering the enclosed survey. By doing so, you will let us know how we can best serve you. Also enclosed is a 10 percent-off coupon to use on your next order to thank you for your time. I'll call you on Wednesday to ask your opinions concerning the survey.

Background Information

Added Service

We value people like you who are willing to take their time to help us serve our customers better. Thanks for all your help.

Thank You

Sincerely yours,

Signature

Jack Larimer
Sales Manager, 800-555-3590

JKL:jiw
Enc.

P.S. The coupon is good now!

Postscript

5

Sales Follow-Up

This letter is used to follow up on a sale that has been made. It may be a thank you for the business, a clarification of the sale or a pitch for future sales.

5

Unlimited View
1854 Vision Lane • Arlington, TX 76016

February 15, 20XX

Marlene T. Thompson
Director of Sales
Omni-Optical Co.
334 S. 114th Avenue
Dallas, TX 75218

Dear Ms. Thompson:

Congratulations on your outstanding sales during our recent winter campaign. Omni-Optical sold 23 percent of our total volume during this program. Please commend your sales staff for their impressive efforts.

Because of your success, you now qualify for our quantity discount. Thanks again for your efforts. We look forward to sharing future sales successes with Omni-Optical.

Sincerely,

Signature

J. Kelly Bandman
Sales Representative

JKB:yek

Statement of Sales

Request

Added Service
Thank You
Goodwill

5

Confirming Sales Order

The following two letters confirm sales taken over the telephone. They offer another opportunity to mention the qualities of the product and make contact with the customer.

Mom's Magic
1121 Elm Avenue
Joplin, MO 64804

June 18, 20XX

Ellen Rhymer
Make Believe Catalog Company
P.O. Box 5217
Amity, OR 97101

Dear Ms. Rhymer:

Thank you for your order of 200 Treasure Trunks from Mom's Magic. I believe you will be very satisfied with the quality of costume pieces included in each. It is this quality which makes my imaginative play apparel so unique.

Thank You
Benefit

As we discussed, I will be shipping 125 storybook trunks and 75 professional trunks to be received no later than August 1. I will be contacting you the week of October 1 to determine if additional trunks are needed. If you need to place an order before then, please call me at 913-555-6215.

Confirmation

Contact Information

Thank you again.

Sincerely,

Signature

Jennifer Lewis

5

Maximum Sales, Inc.
555 West Access Road
Columbia, MO 65217

March 14, 20XX

Andrew Roberts, President
University Sports
468 Baltimore
Kansas City, MO 64105

Dear Mr. Roberts:

This is to confirm your phone order made March 14 for 10,   *Confirmation*
50-count cases of mini-flying disks in fluorescent colors
(green, yellow and pink) to be delivered no later than May 1,   *Details*
20XX. Your logo, a copy of which is enclosed, will be
printed on each disk in black ink.

Thank you for placing an order with Maximum Sales. I   *Goodwill*
understand that these flying disks will be included in the
registration packets of all participants at the Mid-America   *Benefit*
Soccerama scheduled for Memorial Day weekend. I believe
you will be pleased with the increase in sales and name
recognition that will result due to this marketing promotion.

We look forward to being of service to you in the future.   *Complimentary Close*

Sincerely,

Signature

Lisa Nixon
Sales Consultant

Reminder That a Sale Is About to End

Remind a customer that a sale or sales campaign is about to end.

Myrna's Furniture Mart
709 Downey Road • Wiltonshire, NH 03068

April 25, 20XX

Grant W. Werner
Rural Habitats
R.R. 3
Wiltonshire, NH 03104

Dear Mr. Werner:

It hardly seems possible, but there is only one week left in our annual Eastertide Sale. Our letter announcing the sale arrived four weeks ago. It seems like yesterday.

First Reminder

It's still not too late to take advantage of this gigantic sale. The prices this last week are being slashed in half. Come in and take a look at what we have to offer. Our entire sales staff is ready to work with you and Rural Habitats.

Review

Added Service

Attached is our Eastertide Sale flyer. Please take time to look it over and then come see us. You will be glad you did.

Second Reminder

Sincerely,

Signature

Myrna L. Meyerhoff
Sales Manager

MLM:kwn
Enc.

P.S. See the special offer on Page 2 of the flyer!

5

Announcing a Sales Campaign, Promotion or Incentive Program

This type of letter informs clients of upcoming sales promotions, incentive programs or special sales packages that are available. It is followed by a personal call from the salesperson.

Unlimited View
1854 Vision Lane • Arlington, TX 76016

September 15, 20XX

Marlene T. Thompson
Director of Sales
Omni-Optical Co.
334 S. 114th Ave.
Dallas, TX 75218

Dear Ms. Thompson:

Unlimited View will start its winter sales campaign on November 1. — *Announcement*

In the past, this campaign has enabled Omni-Optical to offer its customers a wide selection of products at very competitive prices. It is an outstanding way to attract new customers and build traffic for your business. I have enclosed a sheet explaining all of the particulars along with our latest catalog. — *Explanation* / *Benefits* / *Added Service*

I will call you within the next 10 days to answer any questions you have about the program and take your order. All orders have to be in by October 15. As always, it is a pleasure working with Omni-Optical. — *Deadline* / *Thank You*

Sincerely yours,

Signature

J. Kelly Bandman
Sales Representative

JKB:yek

Announcing a Sales Campaign to Preferred Customers

Announce a sales campaign to preferred customers, thus giving them a head start in purchasing, or offer them further reduced prices.

5

Green Mountain Antiques Wholesale
Stapleton, VT 05020

January 19, 20XX

Max Castle
Heavenly Daze Antiques
Wiloughby, NH 03308

Dear Mr. Castle:

Green Mountain Antiques Wholesale will hold its Winter Sale February 12-16.   *Announcement*

As a preferred customer, you are invited to attend a pre-sale showing on February 11, with discounts up to 50 percent on specially marked items. We feel this is just one small way that we can repay you for all your business over the years. Our enclosed flyer shows you some of the outstanding values available.

Elaboration

Effective Date

Benefit

Thank you for your business. I hope we will see you on February 11.   *Thank You*

Sincerely,

Signature

Madeline O'Shea

MAO:ser
Enc.

Announcing New Products to a Select Group of Customers

Announce new products to a select group of regular customers. It may be seen as a sales pitch.

Ft. Dodge Appliances
563 Grand Ave. • Ft. Dodge, IA 50569

October 30, 20XX

Caroline M. Ness
R.R. 3
Gowrie, IA 50337

Dear Ms. Ness:

Ft. Dodge Appliances is pleased to announce our new line of Wonder Work Appliances. We are now the authorized Wonder Work dealer for Ft. Dodge.

Announcement

Wonder Work Appliances, established for three decades in the East, is now expanding to the Midwest, and we are excited to be part of its expanding network. It specializes in small appliances that are known throughout the industry for their quality and durability. So that you may have a chance to see the appliances at work, we have arranged to demonstrate them this Saturday, November 3, at our store from 9 a.m. to 5 p.m. Special discounts are available if you bring this letter.

Elaboration

Added Service

Benefits

Thank you for your continued business. We look forward to seeing you this Saturday.

Thank You

Sincerely,

Signature

Barney Carlson

BAC:eeo

Announcing a Price Increase

Announce a price increase and soften the blow to the customer.

Grand Greetings, Inc.
330 Big Bend St. • Charleston, SC 29410

February 22, 20XX

Harry C. Marker
Card Distributors, Ltd.
11 Fillmore
Atlanta, GA 30325

Dear Mr. Marker:

Your satisfaction is important to us. In order to continue to produce a high-quality product, we have recently installed new high-speed, high-definition printing presses. This, along with the increased price of paper, has forced us to increase our prices by 10 percent effective March 15. I have enclosed a brochure with the new prices in it for your benefit. Orders received before March 15 will be filled at current prices.

Goal of Customer Satisfaction

Announcement

Incentive

Thank you for your understanding in this matter. We feel that these increases will still allow you to sell these superb cards at competitive prices. We hope you will let us know immediately if there is any way we can serve you better.

Thank You

Goodwill

Sincerely,

Signature

K. Charles Grand
President

KCG:lpw
Enc.

5

Transmittal With Instructions

Complicated instructions can be handled in a cover letter such as this one. Part of each sale is to get the reader/buyer to perform an action that brings him closer to the close of the sale or resale.

5

Zarcon Laser Systems
80000 Orange Blossom Dr.
Boston, MA 02174

March 15, 20XX

Tony Blumenthal, Realtor
The Winstead Building, Suite 400
P.O. Box 46758
Boston, MA 02180

Dear Tony:

Two copies of the revised six-month leasing agreement for the Zarcon Laser Copier II are enclosed. I'm pleased you are happy with its performance.

Purpose
Enclosures

The yellow highlights on one copy reflect the changes that we addressed in our March 14 conversation. Please indicate any additions or omissions in the margins and initial and date each correction. I will review the copy and get back to you by April 5.

Instruction

If the current changes meet with your approval, please sign at the "X" on page 3 of the unmarked copy and return it in the SASE by March 29.

Alternate Instruction

If I may clarify or help in any other way, Tony, please call me at 555-3993.

Contact Information

Sincerely,

Signature

Lee Webster
Senior Account Executive

Enc.

Transmittal With Request

When you must send material and make a request for other material, use a cover letter such as this. Each exchange of information is part of the sales strategy. Keep all technical discussions brief in the letter, with further explanation in the enclosures.

5

Rocky Flats Physics Facility
2367 Central Avenue
Albuquerque, NM 87106

February 16, 20XX

Joseph P. Harlow, Ph.D.
Defense Engineering
784 Trinity Dr.
Los Alamos, NM 87544

Dear Dr. Harlow:

Your inquiry regarding our services is welcome. I am enclosing a brochure that will summarize our optics program for infrared conductors and the surface lab work we do.

Response to Inquiry

If you will send us similar literature from your agency, I can be more specific about what we can do for you.

Request
Benefit

I will call you later this week to answer any questions. Thank you for your interest.

Contact Information

Sincerely,

Signature

Zack A. Bromley, Ph.D.

Enc.

Transmittal With Suggestion

This letter covers technical information briefly and refers to additional service possibilities. Again, allow the enclosures to handle the details of technical material. Use the cover letter to summarize or highlight only.

William Hennings Accountants
Drawer NN
Burlington, NC 27216

December 10, 20XX

Linda Maple
77 Cherry Brook Terr.
Burlington, NC 27218

Dear Linda:

Your projection for the possible Grantor-Retained Income Trust (GRIT) is included with this letter.

Response to Request

You may also want to investigate Grantor-Retained Annuity Trusts (GRATs) and Grantor-Retained Unitrusts (GRUTs). I have taken the liberty of including a pamphlet describing these options in more detail.

Added Service

Please let me know if I may clarify anything for you. We could meet anytime next Thursday at your convenience to discuss which trusts best suit your assets and family situation.

Assistance Offer

Sincerely,

Signature

Davis C. Cernicek

Enc.

Transmittal With Information

A thank-you/sales letter to a client that includes requested information provides ongoing client contact.

Roger Publications Inc.
8560 College Blvd.
Overland Park, KS 66210

September 21, 20XX

Janet Kirby
Alvarez Advertising
10253 W. Higgins Road, Suite 600
Rosemont, IL 60018

Dear Janet:

You made a wise decision by including *Working Women's Guide* in your marketing plans for Mor-PEP! Thank you for your order. — *Goodwill*

Working Women's Guide provides the most effective way to reach this big-volume market. Readership is unexcelled, as shown by the recent Starch WOMEN'S Study. — *Benefit*

Regarding your question on a preprinted insert card: The investment involved is $3,000. If you would like for us to print a card, the card would be a net cost of $1,575. There would be no real cost advantage to using a card attached to our reader service coupon. The cost for the coupon space is $5,000 and includes the printing. Having your message on the card next to the reader service coupon could be a big advantage, however, for readership. — *Information* / *Benefit*

I'll call your office next week to answer any questions on this — and thanks again for your order. — *Contact Information*

Rebecca Ruddy
Account Supervisor

Transmittals With Sales Information

This is a sales letter to a client enclosing promised information.

5

FITZ ADVERTISING, INC.
7592 Front Street
Phoenix, AZ 99065

August 10, 20XX

Robert J. Lee
Powell Glove Company
P.O. Box 5846
Phoenix, AZ 99065

Dear Rob:

How many distributors of work gloves are there? The charts | *Reason*
I promised are enclosed.

Along with the charts, I have included information on the | *Added Service*
availability of the top-distributor summaries and the work
glove management study. These are "hot off the press" —
as of yesterday — and deserve a close look.

Please select the information you want. I can either send it or | *Contact Information*
go over it with you.

I look forward to hearing from you.

Best regards,

Signature

Richard A. Parker

RP/lm

Enc.

This sales letter also serves as a cover letter for enclosed brochures.

United Commercial Bank
P.O. Box 5700
Ukiah, CA 95482

September 14, 20XX

Steven R. Bishop, President
SRB Consulting
P.O. Box 135
Ukiah, CA 95482

Dear Mr. Bishop:

Thank you for your interest in our bank's Small Business Banking Service (SBBS). I certainly enjoyed the opportunity to visit with you Tuesday afternoon. *Goodwill*

As I mentioned, SBBS is designed to meet the special banking needs of the small-business owner. We have packaged a number of popular services under the SBBS umbrella — including free regular checking account, complimentary personalized checks and a standard safe deposit box. *Purpose* *Benefit*

Enclosed is an SBBS brochure listing our services; I have highlighted in yellow those you inquired about. And with this brochure, I have also included several others on the bank and its offerings. *Enclosures*

I will call your office next week to answer any questions you may have and to discuss how United Commercial Bank can best serve you and your consulting company. *Contact Information*

Sincerely,

Signature

Michael Warren

MW:kr

Enc.

Transmittal to Current Client

A cover/sales letter to an existing client, this letter instills a sense of client support from the writer.

5

Roger Publications Inc.
8560 College Blvd.
Overland Park, KS 66210

September 21, 20XX

Joan Morris
NWTC Advertising
P.O. Box 27308
Madison, WI 53707

Dear Joan:

As you mentioned Tuesday, identifying the exact number of working women — single, married, with children and those without children — in today's market is not an easy task. That's why Roger Publications is constantly working to keep you informed about projected industry trends and changes when U.S. Census data becomes outdated. *Benefit*

Finding a unique approach that will influence these key customers is a challenge, also. The *Working Women's Guide* figures (attached) are designed to give you insight and information to make your job easier. *Purpose*

Support

I hope this information continues to help you make key marketing decisions for both AMC and Verasweet. *Emphasis on Benefit*

Best regards,

Signature

Rebecca Ruddy
Account Supervisor

P.S. Thank you for AMC and Verasweet's continued support for Roger Publications. *Thank You Goodwill*

Checklist

- Did you use a positive tone?
- Does the letter sell itself?
- Did you introduce the topic of the letter in the first part?
- Did you mention the recipient's accomplishment or benefit early?
- Did you include all of the necessary details for the client such as date, time and place of appointment?
- Did you include a telephone number so the client can reach you?
- Did you take the initiative in the letter for the action you desire?
- Did you include all background information, added service or details necessary in the second part of the letter so the client understands the letter?
- Did you summarize, thank or recongratulate in the last part of the letter?
- If you received the letter, would you do what you are asking the recipient to do?

Goodwill Letters

This chapter has sample letters to help you write goodwill letters. The broad categories are Professional Recognition and Company Position. These letters identify special events, achievements and issues.

Professional Recognition includes:

- Recognizing a Suggestion
- Appreciation
- Official Anniversary
- Speech
- Invitations
- Congratulations
- Thanks for Good Work: Outside Vendor
- Acknowledging an Accomplishment
- Follow-Up After a Sale

Company Position includes:

- Explaining Policy and Position
- Encouragement
- Announcing New Fringe Benefits
- Adjustment

Other goodwill letters follow in Chapters 7 and 8.

At the side of the page, you will find a brief explanation of each part of the letter. The first letter identifies each section of the letter. Subsequent letters will identify only changes to the basic format.

Step-by-Step Guide

These letters are designed to promote goodwill among clients and employees.

Step 1: The first part of the letter states your purpose. Depending on the reason for writing the letter, this may vary from complimenting an employee on an accomplishment to apologizing for being unable to attend a social event.

Step 2: The second part of the letter gives the details or background information for the first part. This may be anything from explaining to a client the action required to correct a problem to giving details about a social event.

Step 3: The last part of the letter acts as a summary, reminding the recipient of the general nature of the letter. It may be a thank you, or it may restate what has been said in the first part of the letter. For example, if the letter is congratulatory, the last part recongratulates the recipient.

Note: At the end of this chapter is a checklist to use when you write a goodwill letter.

Recognizing a Suggestion

This letter recognizes an employee or business associate for suggestions she has made. Recognition fulfills one of your employees' or associates' greatest personal needs. Use these letters often.

Zimmerman's Resort Highway 131 • Moose Lake, MN 55438	*Letterhead*
June 30, 20XX	*Date*
Maxine Moehlmann Box 25 Moose Lake, MN 55438	*Inside Address*
Dear Maxine:	*Salutation*
Thank you for your great suggestion on how to organize the annual fish fry at Zimmerman's. Your idea means we can serve 100 more people than we did last year. Without a doubt, it is the single best idea that I've seen in a long time.	*First Thanks*
As you know, Zimmerman's motto is "Fun for All," and as a reward for your suggestion, we are giving you a daylong pass to Valley Faire in Shakopee, Minnesota, for you and your family. We hope you all can live up to Zimmerman's motto.	*General Statement About Company (optional)* *Benefit*
Thank you once again for your great idea. With employees like you, Zimmerman's will only get better.	*Second Thanks (optional)*
Sincerely,	*Complimentary Close*
Signature	*Signature*
Sally Zimmerman President	*Typed Name*
SJZ:dft	*Additional Information*

Appreciation

This letter expresses appreciation for something that was done. Quite often these letters are to employees of a company. Thank-you notes are meaningful rewards. The written word has power.

6

Seven Sisters
709 Starry Way • Council Bluffs, IA 50574

April 13, 20XX

R.K. Kirkman
4590 N. Iowa Avenue
Omaha, NE 68164

Dear Mr. Kirkman:

On behalf of the staff at Seven Sisters, I want to express my appreciation for your help in our recent ad campaign. Your tireless efforts made the campaign one of the most successful we have ever had.

Reason for Appreciation

Seven Sisters' success relies heavily on the commitment of its employees. Devotion such as yours allows us to be leaders in the field of fashion merchandising in the Omaha/Council Bluffs area. Your efforts contribute to higher sales, and that, as you know, means increased profit-sharing for our employees.

General Statement About the Company

Specific Recognition

Thank you for all of your hard work. Seven Sisters is successful because of employees like you.

Thank You

Sincerely,

Signature

Laney Moore
President

LAM:rie

Official Anniversary

This letter recognizes an official anniversary, such as the ordination of a priest or minister, an elected official taking office or an employee's work anniversary. It elevates morale.

Wood Hollow Cranberries
850 Random Rd. • New London, CT 06320

April 8, 20XX

Edward Brown
8879 Kirksville Ct.
New London, CT 06320

Dear Ed:

All of us at Wood Hollow Cranberries wish to extend our sincerest congratulations on your 10th anniversary here at Wood Hollow. Your work, first as assistant plant manager and now as plant manager, has been exemplary. We are most pleased to have you on our management team and look forward to many more years of working with you.

Sincerely yours,

Signature

Grace Kleissman
President

GWK:gmn

Congratulations

Specific Positions

Goodwill

6

Speech

This letter acknowledges a speech the recipient gave and comments on it.

Calvin Coolidge High School
3222 25th St., N.E. • Minot, ND 58504

May 23, 20XX

Barbara Rundle, Principal
Lake of the Woods High School
Box 66
Lake of the Woods, MN 20902

Dear Ms. Rundle:

I recently attended the North Central States Principals' Convention in Fargo and heard your speech on problems in the rural high school. I was most impressed and came away with many new ideas and insights.

I was particularly interested in your discussion of college preparation in the rural school. Although Calvin Coolidge High School does not qualify as a rural school, it has many of the same problems. An author I've found most enlightening who deals with rural schools is Garret Randolf. His works, *Rural America: Who's Educating You?* and *One Room Schools Grown Up*, are both excellent. Are you aware of these titles? They weren't on your bibliography.

I shall look forward to your speech in Pierre, as I see you are on the program.

Sincerely,

Signature

C. Max Hanks
Principal

CMH:bar

Acknowledgment of Speech

Comments About the Speech

Additional Service

Expectation

Invitation — Formal

This letter's formal language reflects the formality of the event. It requires a formal reply.

Erskins and Co.
985 Washington • Boise, ID 83805
555-8800

October 1, 20XX

Carmen and Ted Schmitt
800 Lander Lane
Meridian, ID 83642

Dear Mr. and Mrs. Schmitt:

You are cordially invited to a formal dinner in honor of Samuel Whitters on October 21, 20XX, at 8 p.m. at the Boise Hilton.

Time, Date and Place of Event

Mrs. Schmitt, as you are an associate of Mr. Whitters, we would like you to speak briefly about his work in the lumber industry. If this is possible, please let me know within the next week.

Request

Deadline

Please note that this is a black-tie event. RSVP with the names of those attending by October 14.

Requirements

Sincerely yours,

Signature

John Randall III
Chairman, Social Committee

JKR:sat

6

Invitation — Informal

This letter is more informal and conversational in style. It may require a reply, but the reply may be oral or informally written.

TeleWorld
1810 Ohio Ave. • Little Rock, AR 72293

June 13, 20XX

Ramona Jenkins
55 Tremont
Little Rock, AR 72291

Dear Ramona:

The marketing department is having a surprise get-together next Thursday afternoon after work for the retirement of J.J. Small.

Time, Date and Place of Event

Please bring a gag gift to send J.J. on her way to a happy retirement. We're asking each person to contribute $5 for a legitimate retirement gift. Wanda Templeman is collecting.

Requests

Let Wanda (ext. 233) know by Monday if you can make it, so she can order enough refreshments.

Requirements Deadline

Sincerely,

Signature

Chuck Meyers
Chairman, Social Committee

CJM:eem

Congratulations

This is a goodwill letter on the part of the company or the salesperson to a client. It congratulates an internal client on an accomplishment.

Capital Life Insurance Co.
369 Wilmington Blvd. • Camden, NJ 07102

May 7, 20XX

Seth Tinkerton Jr.
District Manager
839 Littleton Ct.
Morningside, NJ 07112

Dear Mr. Tinkerton:

Congratulations on being the top district manager for March and April. You can be proud of your hard work, and we're glad you work with us.

Acknowledgment of Accomplishment

Capital Life honors its high achievers with our Call to Excellence Award. Your achievement in sales will be recognized at the June Convention in Philadelphia. We would like you and your agents to be our guests at a special banquet on June 5, 20XX, at 7:30 p.m. in the Cameo Room of the Hotel International, during which you will receive the award.

General Statement About Achievement

Specific Details

Once again, congratulations! It is because of managers like you that Capital Life has achieved the success it enjoys.

Restatement

Sincerely yours,

Signature

John R. Liu
Vice President

JRL:cco

This congratulates a good worker and encourages success for the next task.

FRANKLIN & FRANKLIN ADVERTISING
14 South Fremont St.
Suite 1310
Grand Terrace, CA 92313

Sender's Address

October 11, 20XX

Karen Winters
11850 Mount Vernon Ave.
Grand Terrace, CA 92313

Dear Karen:

Congratulations on being awarded the Blanding Foods account. You did an excellent job convincing their management that Franklin & Franklin should be the agency to represent their new frozen-food line.

Specifics

The creativity and determination you demonstrated in presenting our company to Blanding Foods will be equally helpful in designing an advertising campaign suited to their needs. Their goal of becoming a leading supplier of frozen desserts to school cafeterias will require an imaginative sales approach.

Future Benefit

I look forward to seeing your continued success in dealing with this important new account.

Encouragement

Sincerely,

Signature

Alan G. Franklin
President

This letter congratulates a friend or business associate on a recent promotion.

West and Associates
11 East 8th St.
Boston, MA 02116

March 13, 20XX

Richard A. Peters
9032 Thompson
Boston, MA 02116

Dear Richard:

Congratulations on your promotion to general manager at Ryan Corporation. You have excellent business skills and the drive to go far — keep up the good work!

Purpose

I'm pleased the management at Ryan recognizes your abilities.

Personal Comment

Best wishes for many future successes.

Goodwill

Sincerely,

Signature

Pat Monroe

Thanks for Good Work:
Outside Vendor

This letter expresses appreciation for good work. It serves as a cover letter for workshop material.

6

Addison Manufacturing
P.O. Box 5310
Boulder, CO 80322

June 1, 20XX

Sharon Young
Right On! Writing
P.O. Box 6864
Boulder, CO 80322

Dear Sharon:

Enclosed is a summary of the evaluations from the accelerated reading course. We are very pleased with the results and feel you met our expectations with a difficult topic quite well.

Reason
Appreciation

It has been a pleasure working with you. Sorry that I missed the last meeting of the group.

Goodwill

Thank you for tailoring the course and using our own materials so that company objectives were met.

Thank You
Specific Details

Sincerely,

Signature

Elizabeth Davis
Supervisor, Purchasing Services

Enc.

Acknowledging Accomplishments

In this letter, an employer recognizes a good idea of an employee and mentions the positive comments of others as well.

Baker's Department Store
432 Washington Ave.
Independence, MO 64052

December 12, 20XX

Sharon Rash
2508 East Elm
Independence, MO 64053

Dear Sharon:

You are doing a super job and it shows! Because of your efforts in coordinating the seasonal decorations around one theme, each department looks better — and that has the entire store looking better. And, of course, this makes it a more pleasant place to work for all of us.

Appreciation

Your efforts have been noticed not only by staff but also by our customers. Several have mentioned the "new" look. The extra time you spent on this project is greatly appreciated; the enclosed is our "Thank you for a good idea and a job well done."

Specifics

Enclosure

Sincerely,

Signature

Steven Baker
President

Enc.

This letter thanks a staff member for a job done well.

Schwartz Manufacturing Company
P.O. Box 3732
Secaucus, NJ 07096

April 7, 20XX

Jennifer Matthews
819 Brookline Ave.
Secaucus, NJ 07096

Dear Jennifer:

Thank you for the excellent job you did in preparing and presenting the quarterly report! It was evident to me and to the group that you had put a lot of time and thought into its preparation. The handouts especially contained very useful information, and you covered in your presentation all the points you and I had discussed beforehand.

Your contribution to the success of Schwartz Manufacturing is greatly appreciated!

Sincerely,

Signature

Robert Gramlich
President

RG:pd

Thank You

Specific Details

Goodwill

This thank-you letter to an employee is specific. The letter gives details as to why the bonus and the recognition were earned.

A Better Bookstore
499 West Eighth Street
Aurora, CO 80010

November 12, 20XX

Sheila Martin
1422 Cramer Ave.
Denver, CO 80121

Dear Sheila:

Thank you for the extra amount of time and effort you spent to ensure that A Better Bookstore was successfully represented at this year's Mountain State Professional Reading Teachers' Conference. A check is enclosed as recognition of your superior work.

Specific Situation

Reward

The sales of reading materials for elementary-age students was 20 percent higher than we anticipated. More importantly, I am confident that A Better Bookstore has gained new customers, due to your knowledge of the materials for sale and your emphasis on individualized attention to each conference participant you assisted.

Specific Details

Congratulations on a job well done.

Goodwill

Sincerely,

Signature

Harry Tellman
Manager

This letter acknowledges an accomplishment of a client, employee, relative of a client or employee, or friend of the company.

6

Pampered Prints
282 Kefauver Dr. • Mt. Vernon, KY 42040

March 30, 20XX

Maria Fernandez
3333 Trenton Way
Mt. Vernon, KY 42049

Dear Maria:

Your design for our Kute Kids line is outstanding! Pampered Prints is proud that you are one of our employees.

Acknowledgment of Accomplishment

Because of your design, Kute Kids is breaking all records in sales. During the first quarter, Kute Kids outsold all other lines in the Size 6-12 category.

General Statement About Achievement

Keep up the good work. We need people like you, Maria, at Pampered Prints.

Encouragement

Sincerely yours,

Signature

Lily Marret
Director of Sales

LNM:ddl

Follow-up After a Sale

This letter is a follow-up to an event. It maintains positive contact and encourages repeat business from the client.

WAVERLEY HOTEL
360 South Dearborn • Chicago, IL 60604

October 31, 20XX

Cynthia Brown
The First Management Group
110 First Ave.
Clayton, MO 63105

Dear Cynthia:

It was such a pleasure to have a group like yours as our guest! Not only did we enjoy having The First Management Group in our hotel, but also getting to work with you was an added benefit! You are so professional and organized that you make us look good.

Compliment

Goodwill

Cynthia, if there's anything I can ever do to help you, give me a call. Please stay in touch; the next time you're in Chicago, we'll take some time and see the city!

Personal Note

Sincerely,

Signature

Carol Brawn
Director, Convention Services

6

Explaining Policy and Position

This memo clarifies a company's policy and position for its employees. Normally a memo would suffice, but a formal letter may also be appropriate in certain circumstances.

MEMORANDUM

Date: December 23, 20XX
To: All Employees
From: Manuel Gonzales
Re: Policy Concerning Sick Leave

There seems to be some misunderstanding concerning Swithams' sick-leave policy.

Statement of the Situation

Each employee is allowed 10 sick days per year during the first five years of employment. For five to 10 years of employment, each employee is allowed 15 days of sick leave. Any employee of 10 or more years is granted 20 days of sick leave. Sick leave may be accumulated up to one full year (365 days). After an absence of two days, an employee must seek medical advice and present a doctor's excuse upon return to work. Failure to do so may result in docking of pay for any sick leave after two consecutive days. For further information, refer to the employee manual, page 23, or contact our benefits officer, Barbara Wieland.

Clarification

Consequence

I hope this clears up any misunderstanding, particularly concerning the doctor's excuse.

Specific Issue
Goodwill

Encouragement

This letter offers encouragement to the employees of a firm.

6

RM Trucking
8092 Las Noches • Santa Fe, NM 87538
505-555-0050

December 12, 20XX

Cappy Kappmeier
Wind Willow 13
Santa Fe, NM 87538

Dear Cappy:

Every year I take time to look ahead to what the next year has in store for our employees. Next year's outlook is exciting.

Purpose

In the past year, RM Trucking has experienced phenomenal growth, moving from the tenth-largest trucking firm in New Mexico to the second-largest. We project that in the coming year we will become number one in New Mexico and number two in the combined states of New Mexico and Arizona. It is because of our farsighted staff that we have been able to achieve this kind of success. Naturally, this success affects everyone who works for RM Trucking. Because of our unique profit-sharing plan, each employee benefits.

Explanation of the Purpose

Benefits

Next year will be exciting at RM for all of us involved. I hope you will make the most of these opportunities.

Restatement Encouragement

Sincerely,

Signature

Ronald Martin
President

RMM:wan

Announcing New Fringe Benefits

This letter announces new fringe benefits to employees of a company.

Warwick Manufacturing
1500 Burnside Parkway • Warwick, RI 02891

August 24, 20XX

Glenn Golden
90 Wuthering Heights Dr.
Kingston, RI 02881

Dear Mr. Golden:

It is my pleasure to announce that Warwick Manufacturing is offering a new employee benefit plan starting January 1.   *Announcement*

After much discussion with management and labor, we have settled on a plan that allows you to choose those benefits you want and need. The enclosed brochure outlines the complete program. We are excited about it because you will have total control over your benefits.   *Explanation*

Enclosure

Please call Sally Martin in the Human Resources Department if you have any questions or concerns.   *Contact Information*

We hope that you will be pleased with this new benefit package.   *Closing Statement*

Sincerely,

Signature

Susanna M. Graham
President

SMG:eer

Adjustment

This letter requests an adjustment, either business or social, and asks for the understanding of the person for whom the adjustment is being asked.

Australian Outfitters
P.O. Box 212 • Los Angeles, CA 99045-0212

October 3, 20XX

Corinne Reynolds
3510 Aroya Canyon Road
Hollywood Hills, CA 95234

Dear Ms. Reynolds:

I regret to inform you that your order of boomerangs will be delayed by four weeks because of a recent fire at Outback Boomerangs in Sydney, Australia. | *Apology*
Reason

I hope this delay is acceptable. As soon as we found out about the fire, we contacted Woolabang Boomerangs in Alice Springs and were able to fill your order. Unfortunately, its boomerangs take longer to make because they are handmade. This is to your advantage: Though they are more expensive, we will absorb the difference in cost. | *Explanation*

Benefit

Thank you for your understanding and cooperation in this unfortunate matter. If you have any questions, please call me at 800-OUTBACK. | *Thanks*

Sincerely yours,

Signature

Tanner Dundee

TJD:mal

6

Checklist

- Did you use a pleasant tone in the letter?
- Did you state the purpose of the letter in the first part?
- Did you give background and details in the second part to further explain the first part?
- Did you summarize the letter in the last part?
- Is the letter sincere?
- Did you personalize the letter so that it doesn't sound institutional?
- Does the letter express goodwill?
- If you received the letter, would you feel good about it?

*C*HAPTER 7

Community Activities Letters

This chapter has sample letters dealing with community activities. The broad categories are as follows:

- Solicitation of Funds
- Acknowledgment and Request for Funds
- Appreciation and Fund-Raising Event
- Acknowledgment of Contribution
- Acknowledgment of Accomplishment
- Thank You
- Grant Request
- Invitation to Serve
- Membership Invitation
- Refusal of a Request
- Expression of Appreciation
- Appointment to Office
- Appointment to a Committee
- Compliment
- Invitation to Speak
- Complimenting a Speaker
- Letter to Legislator Showing Support
- Letter to Legislator Showing Concern

At the side of the page, you will find a brief explanation of each part of the letter. The first letter identifies each section of the letter. Subsequent letters identify only changes to the basic format.

Step-by-Step Guide

These letters address community activities that involve both individuals and corporations.

Step 1: The first part of the letter states your purpose. It may vary from asking a company to take part in a charity fund-raising drive to expressing appreciation for an employee's involvement in the community.

Step 2: The second part of the letter gives the details or background information for the first part. This may include giving a reason for declining a public office to indicating your company's policy about an employee's achievement.

Step 3: The last part of the letter acts as a summary, reminding the recipient of the general nature of the letter. It may include deadlines, a thank you, or a re-request.

Note: At the end of this chapter is a checklist to use when you write a community activities letter.

Solicitation of Funds

This letter requests that a company contribute to a charity.

JJT: Heavy Equipment 1288 E. U.S. 63 • Sioux City, IA 50585	*Letterhead*
April 9, 20XX	*Date*
William J. Buchheit President Sanders and Thoms 348 Lincolnway Dr. South Sioux City, IA 50585	*Inside Address*
Dear Mr. Buchheit:	*Salutation*
The United Benefit for Community Improvement is starting its annual drive this Monday. We hope you will contribute to this worthy cause.	*Request*
In the past, Sanders and Thoms has been one of the leaders in the UBCI drive, with its employees giving an average of 2.5 percent of their income to the fund. Naturally, they recognize that the fund improves their lives as well as the lives of others in the area. May we count on your corporate support again? This year we are asking each corporation to match its employees' contributions.	*Support or Background Information* *Recognition*
Your contributions provide recreation scholarships to summer and after-school programs for youth, home maintenance assistance for the elderly, AIDS education, a community pantry and kitchen, and other programs for community improvement.	*Benefit*
Please continue your leadership in community development through your support of UBCI. We are asking that all contributions, employee and corporate, be in the UBCI office, 3001 Carrington Way, Sioux City, Iowa 56884, by May 15. Thank you for your continued support.	*Re-request,* *Deadline and Thanks*
Sincerely yours,	*Complimentary Close*
Signature	*Signature*
Lannie Miller Campaign Chairperson	*Typed Name*
LJM:wit	*Additional Information*

An initial information letter is necessary to introduce the non-profit organization to the reader. The information should appeal to both the emotion and intellect for the greatest impact.

Haven Home
P.O. Box 124 • Memphis, TN 38124

March 12, 20XX

Dear Friend,

Jenny Louise is 12 years old. Her parents argued last month. The shotgun blast ignited the heater, and her father died in the explosion. Her mother is still hospitalized with severe burns. Jenny Louise was lucky — at least physically. She was placed at Haven Home because no foster parents are available to care for her now. Our community resources are stretched to capacity. | *Story*

Thousands of children face the consequences of domestic violence each day. Families suffer, children cry and people die. Unresolved, unrestrained anger is at epidemic proportions in most urban communities today. Memphis is included. Within the past 12 months, Haven Home has received 3,122 crisis calls, sheltered 738 individuals and educated 20,493 concerned people. | *Statistics*

Individuals like Jenny Louise who seek our help need *your* help. Please consider a donation of time or money — or both. No matter how much of either you have, you have more of each than those at Haven Home. | *Appeal for Volunteers and Funds*

Time: Apply to be a foster parent through the state human resources agencies. Call us for information or an appointment to contribute your time as a volunteer at Haven Home.

Money: $20 pays one person's meals for a day; $50 pays a week's utilities; $100 trains an adult in anger control or prepares a person for the G.E.D.

Send as much as you can now. Together we can make a difference!

Sincerely,

Signature

Anna Phelps
Executive Director

AP:sfg

P.S. Make your tax-deductible check payable to Haven Home. Thank you! | *Postscript*

Acknowledgment and Request for Funds

Follow-up letters provide a nonprofit organization the opportunity to thank a contributor and to suggest future contributions.

Haven Home
P.O. Box 124 • Memphis, TN 38124

March 25, 20XX

Dan Pearson
278 Briarwell St.
Memphis, TN 38121

Dear Dan:

Thank you for your generous donation. Your contribution of $50 will enable us to continue helping our community fight against domestic violence.

Thank You

Acknowledgment

Would you consider giving Haven Home a monthly donation of $50? Our needs continue throughout the year, and we count on the generosity of people such as you, Dan. Other ways you might consider to help us secure our programs for the future include memorials, trusts, scholarships and bequests. With your financial support and our dedicated volunteers, Haven Home can continue to serve victims of domestic violence with high-quality intervention programs.

Continuing Need and Appeal

Again, thank you for your support.

Second Thank You

Sincerely,

Signature

Anna Phelps
Executive Director

AP:sfg

7

Appreciation and Fund-Raising Event

Contributors want to know how their dollars are used. Updating a previous story is one way to show value. Another way is through an appreciation event that may or may not be connected to additional fund raising.

Haven Home
P.O. Box 124 • Memphis, TN 38124

May 5, 20XX

Dan Pearson
278 Briarwell St.
Memphis, TN 38121

Dear Dan:

Thank you! Your pledge for $25 each month for a year is greatly appreciated.

Thanks
Appreciation

You asked about an update regarding Jenny Louise: She and her mother are now living with her maternal grandmother, and the investigation around the explosion continues. Thank you for your concern.

Specific
Response

Many people have expressed their concern and commitment to stop domestic violence through their pledges and gifts. Some have volunteered as a result. The board, staff, volunteers and residents at Haven Home want to thank you in person. Please join us for an appreciation dinner supported by:

Suggestions

Appreciation

Georgio's Fine Italian Restaurant
at 39th Street and Knoll
on Thursday, May 23, 20XX, at 7:30 p.m.

Event Details

A silent auction will follow dinner. Retail stores at the Galla Center are donating items for our event. We would be delighted to have you attend.

Fund-Raising
Event

As always, thank you for your help.

Thanks

Sincerely,

Signature

Anna Phelps
Executive Director
AP:sfg
RSVP by May 20 at 555-3883. See you there!

RSVP

Acknowledgment of Contribution

This letter acknowledges that a company has contributed to a charity.

JJT: Heavy Equipment
1288 E. U.S. 63 • Sioux City, IA 50585

April 25, 20XX

William J. Buchheit
President
Sanders and Thoms
348 Lincolnway Drive
South Sioux City, IA 50585

Dear Mr. Buchheit:

The United Benefit for Community Improvement would like to thank you and your employees for your generous contribution to this year's fund drive. Your contribution of $99,751 is the largest corporate/employee contribution so far.

First Acknowledgment of the Contribution

Donna Truemper, your UBCI chairperson, will let the employees of Sanders and Thoms know of their accomplishment. This year they gave an average of 2.75 percent of their income to the fund. Their contribution and yours will definitely help us meet our goal of $2 million.

General Statement About the Contribution

Specific Details

All of you at Sanders and Thoms are to be commended for your generosity. Thank you again for your contribution.

Second Acknowledgment

Sincerely yours,

Signature

Lannie Miller
Campaign Chairperson

LJM:wit

7

Acknowledgment of Accomplishment

This letter expresses goodwill and acknowledges an accomplishment by someone who has a relationship to the company (employee, relative of an employee, friend of the company).

KJZ, Inc.
45 Western Hills Rd. • St. Paul, MN 55445

July 28, 20XX

Jake Tillis
R.R. 1
Lake Woebegone, MN 56151

Dear Mr. Tillis:

KJZ is proud to have the new Twin Cities Corporate 10K Marathon winner on its staff. Your performance in Saturday's run was impressive.

It was most thrilling to see you cross the finish line wearing your KJZ T-shirt and then watch the performance again on the evening news. Your hard work and training have paid off. The corporate trophy was the result of your accomplishment.

The trophy will be prominently displayed in the front lobby at KJZ. Thank you for representing us so ably.

Sincerely,

Signature

Kevin J. Zimmerman
President

KJZ:rmz

Accomplishment
First Acknowledgment

General Statement
About the
Accomplishment

Second
Acknowledgment
Thank You

Thank You

Similar to the letter expressing appreciation, this letter thanks an employee or business associate for something he has done.

King's Court Auto
1500 Wright Way • Kitty Hawk, NC 27831

November 17, 20XX

Lee Kim Park
23 Timberline Dr.
Tarryton, NC 27789

Dear Mr. Park:

On behalf of the management at King's Court Auto, I would like to thank you for your recent participation in the United Way Campaign as Region 7's Unit Leader.

First Thank You

Your leadership in the United Way not only helps the community but also reflects well on King's Court Auto. Civic participation is important, and we are proud of our employees when they take part in the community.

General Comments

Encouragement

Thank you once again for all your hard work. Hats off to you!

Second Thank You

Sincerely yours,

Signature

Donald King
Chairman of the Board

DSK:hey

Grant Request

Although most grant requests require a specific application form, you still need to send a cover letter with the form. This letter is a sample cover letter.

Salina Community College
45 Cottonwood Dr. • Salina, KS 67401

October 14, 20XX

Carl L. Meyerhoff
Director of Grants
Salina Area Grant Office
350 First Street
Salina, KS 67401

Dear Mr. Meyerhoff:

We would like to request a $15,000 grant for Salina Community College to improve access for the handicapped. I have enclosed our grant application.

The majority of the buildings on the Salina Community College campus were built prior to 1953. Those built after 1945 are accessible to the handicapped. Unfortunately, Atkinson Auditorium, where we hold graduation, monthly convocations and other major events, was built in 1932 and is not accessible to the handicapped. The $15,000 grant would allow us to install ramps at each entrance and remove a row of seats for wheelchairs, making the entire campus accessible to the handicapped.

Thank you for your prompt action on this grant. We shall look forward to hearing from you.

Sincerely yours,

Signature

Mary Ellen Feldman
Director of Physical Facilities

MEF:klo

Request for Grant

Requirements

Background Information and Summary of Need

Thank You

Invitation to Serve

This letter invites someone with the company to serve on a committee or in a position — governmental or charitable.

Greater Pittsburgh Family Fund
760 Allegheny Dr. • Mt. Lebanon, PA 16301

July 1, 20XX

Larry M. Grimschaw
993 White Water Way
Mt. Lebanon, PA 16301

Dear Mr. Grimschaw:

We of the Greater Pittsburgh Family Fund would like to invite you to chair the Health Committee for 20XX. | *Invitation*

The Health Committee disburses funds to help families that have exhausted all other medical resources. We are asking you to chair this committee of eight people for one year. | *Explanation*

Your leadership and organizational skills are essential for our continuing success. As a committee member last year, your dedication to health was apparent. Here is your chance to make a difference in the lives of families in desperate need. We need your combination of compassion and competence in directing the Health Committee. | *Persuasion*

Presently, the committee meets weekly to review requests and act on them. Additionally, you would need to prepare a monthly disbursement report to be presented to the Greater Pittsburgh Family Fund's monthly Steering Committee. You would report directly to me. | *Requirements and Duties*

Thank you for considering this offer. Please let me know by July 15, 20XX, if you are able to take this position. I look forward to working with you. | *Thank You Set Deadline*

Sincerely yours,

Signature

Coretta Marshall
General Chairperson

CAM:tpw

Membership Invitation

Membership drives are common in volunteer organizations. Here is how you can hook your reader and catch a member.

Community Valors
642 Rocky Mountain Road • Denver, CO 80023

September 14, 20XX

Mary E. Marius
866 Aspen Place
Denver, CO 80025

Dear Ms. Marius:

As a new resident of Denver, wouldn't you like to get to know the city and its people better? Then consider the service and networking opportunities Community Valors could provide you. — *Benefit*

We meet monthly to plan service projects that improve life in Denver. You have already seen our trademark red vests on the job at the blood bank where you so generously gave of yourself last Friday. We are always looking for enthusiastic and empathetic people to participate in our organization. We think you meet the qualifications! — *Background*

Some of our projects this past year have included establishing a food and toiletry pantry for people with AIDS, tutoring for people whose second or third language is English, and emergency aid to people suffering from disaster, disease or distress. Each project is funded by membership dues of $90 per year and special contributions from area businesses. — *Projects* / *Dues*

Our annual membership drive began this week and runs through the end of September. We invite you to become part of the largest volunteer service organization in the state. May we call upon you to ask any questions you may have about Community Valors and to encourage you to join our efforts? Please send the enclosed postcard to us now. We promise to serve your interests and find outlets for your talents in Community Valors. — *Invitation* / *Ask for Permission to Contact*

Sincerely,

Signature

Mac Williams and Beth Tomasic
Membership Drive Co-chairs

P.S. Save some time so you can begin sharing your time: Send your membership dues in with the postcard, and we'll get you into a project right away. We have a red vest waiting for you! — *Postscript Invitation*

7

Refusal of a Request

This letter refuses a request made by another company or individual.

Marion Medical Supply
883 Union N.W. • Marion, KY 41503

November 16, 20XX

M.D. Easton
Cranston County Democratic Chairman
995 Rapid Run Rd.
Marion, KY 41503

Dear Mr. Easton:

I regret that I will be unable to run for County Commissioner | *Refusal*
as we discussed last Friday. It is flattering to be asked, but
circumstances do not allow me to run for office at this time.

I am declining because of prior commitments to my family | *Reason*
and my business. I would not have the time to campaign or
to devote to the position because of the prolonged illness of
my mother and the amount of travel required by my
business. I shall continue to actively support the Democratic
Party, through both volunteer efforts and monetary support.

Thank you for considering me. I appreciate your | *Thank You for*
understanding. | *Understanding*

Sincerely yours,

Signature

Duke Snow

DDS:van

Expression of Appreciation

This letter expresses appreciation for an act by an employee or a business associate.

7

Democratic Committee
995 Rapid Run Road • Marion, KY 41503

October 30, 20XX

Duke Snow
Marion Medical Supply
883 Union N.W.
Marion, KY 41503

Dear Mr. Snow:

Thank you for your support in our recent election. Your hard work is greatly appreciated along with your monetary contributions.

Express Appreciation

When you indicated last November that you would not be able to run for commissioner, I was disappointed. But I knew that you would support us in any way possible. Once again, you came through. It was because of your untiring, behind-the-scenes work that we were able to sweep the election. You are essential to Cranston County Democrats.

General Statement About the Situation

Thank you once again for all your hard work. Without you, we couldn't have done it.

Reiterate Appreciation

Sincerely yours,

Signature

M.D. "Doc" Easton
Cranston County Democratic Chairman

MDE:klw

Appointment to Office

This letter congratulates the recipient on his appointment to an office in government or a charitable organization.

Clothier's International
793 W. Washington • Tanville, RI 02878

September 30, 20XX

Samuel R. Grant
1515 Sycamore Lane
Tanville, RI 02878

Dear Sam:

Congratulations on your recent appointment to the Tanville City Council. You should be proud of your accomplishment.

Congratulations

Our policy of civic leave encourages our employees to participate in government. Your longstanding commitment to the community and this recent appointment make us proud to have you on our staff.

General Statement About Company

Specific Recognition

Keep up the good work. We need more people like you looking out for Tanville's interests.

Encouragement (optional)

Sincerely,

Signature

Lisa M. Mannerheim
Assistant Vice President

LMM:jjk

Appointment to a Committee

This letter congratulates an employee or business associate on an appointment to a committee.

Keystone Educational Agency
562 Rolling Hills • Birdsdale, PA 19508

January 10, 20XX

Karen Gorman
Box 67, R.R. 4
New Jerusalem, PA 18825

Dear Karen:

Congratulations on your appointment to the Excellence in Education Committee for Lucas County. We are pleased that one of our staff will be representing us and know that your experience and education will serve you well.

First Congratulations

Striving for excellence in education in the tri-state area is of utmost importance. You have worked hard in the past supporting educational issues, and I'm sure you will continue your strong leadership role in the Excellence in Education Committee for Lucas County.

General Statement (optional)

If you need any help or resources, be sure to let us know. We are proud of your success and know that this appointment will bring you much personal satisfaction.

Second Congratulations (optional)

Sincerely,

Signature

Benjamin K. Douglas
Superintendent

BKD:ssp

Compliment

Similar to letters that congratulate and acknowledge accomplishments, this letter compliments someone (employee, relative of an employee, friend of the company) on something he has done.

Kids World
2255 Wilson Blvd. • Galentine, IL 61036

January 20, 20XX

C.K. Leister
R.R. 5
Galentine, IL 61036

Dear C.K.:

Your fine performance in the Galentine Community Theatre last Friday was noteworthy. You brought Stanley to life in *A Streetcar Named Desire*.

It is exciting for me to see fellow employees involved in the fine arts. I'm sure you are aware that Kids World has been a corporate supporter of the Galentine Community Theatre since its inception.

You are to be commended for your fine interpretation. Keep up the good work.

Sincerely,

Signature

Lorraine J. Black
President

LJB:kkc

First Compliment

Relate to the Company (optional)

Second Compliment (optional)

Invitation to Speak

This letter invites someone from the community to speak at a company-related function.

Enterprises, Ltd.
345 Waconia Rd. • Denver, CO 80023

June 5, 20XX

Leonard Takamoto
5699 Mission Highway
Bismarck, ND 58578

Dear Mr. Takamoto:

We at Enterprises, Ltd. would like to ask you to speak at our Annual Stockholders' Meeting on August 10, 20XX, in Denver.

Your reputation as an entrepreneur in the field of small businesses interests us. As you may know, Enterprises, Ltd. acts as a clearing house for small businesses and supplies ideas and seed money for new small businesses. Your recent article in *Success* speaks to the topic that we would like our stockholders to hear: "The Future of America Lies in Its Small Businesses." We hope you will consider this offer.

Thank you for your time. Attached is a sheet outlining all of the particulars: remuneration, schedules, hotel and airline arrangements. Please let me know by June 15 if you will accept this speaking engagement. You can reach me at 208-555-7793.

Sincerely yours,

Signature

Hal J. Martinson
Executive Administrative Assistant

HJM:lld

Invitation
Meeting Details

Explanation

Specific Topic

Thank You
Attachment
Deadline for Reply
Contact Information

Complimenting a Speaker

This letter compliments a speaker who has spoken at a company-related function.

Enterprises, Ltd.
345 Waconia Rd. • Denver, CO 80023

August 11, 20XX

Leonard Takamoto
5699 Mission Highway
Bismarck, ND 58578

Dear Mr. Takamoto:

On behalf of the stockholders at Enterprises, Ltd., I would like to thank you for your speech yesterday. Several stockholders have called me this morning to say how much they agreed with what you were talking about.

First Compliment

I was particularly pleased to hear that Enterprises, Ltd. is right on target with our mission statement concerning small businesses. The renewal of a solid economic base in the rural areas of the Midwest is the result of forward-looking people such as yourself and our board of directors. Dr. Michael Pearson, one of our largest stockholders, spoke to me this morning and put it succinctly: "Mr. Takamoto hit the nail on the head when he pointed out that the future is in small businesses."

Elaboration (optional)

Testimony

Please send me your expense report for immediate reimbursement. Include copies of receipts and an invoice number to facilitate this transaction.

Thank you for your inspiring speech. It was our privilege to hear you.

Thank You
Second Compliment

Sincerely yours,

Signature

Calvin R. Stiers
President
CRS:est

Letter to Legislator Showing Support

This letter shows support of a bill being considered. The elaboration paragraph builds the writer's credibility and increases the power of the support.

7

Mario's Pasta Inns, Inc.
803 King Ave. • Odessa, TX 76514

September 8, 20XX

The Honorable Sarah Williams
Representative
Government Offices
9900 Ralston Way
Austin, TX 78603

Dear Ms. Williams:

Your continued concern for both restaurant owners and customers is admirable, and H.R. 305 demonstrates that concern. I support H.R. 305, which you recently introduced.

Statement of Support

I own Mario's Pasta Inns, Inc., a chain of 15 Italian restaurants throughout Texas. Additionally, I am the past spokesperson for Restaurateurs International and am an active member of its governing board. We wholeheartedly support your bill that limits the sales tax on meals eaten out. We can see that raising the tax will hurt the owners and our customers.

Elaboration (optional)

Thank you for your concern and your untiring pursuit of keeping taxes in line. You have our support.

Thank You

Sincerely yours,

Signature

Mario Napoli
President

MDN:klu

Letter to Legislator Showing Concern

This letter shows concern over a bill being considered. Although elaboration is still optional in the second paragraph, it builds credibility for the writer's opinion and offers a persuasive comparison. This paragraph cannot be discounted easily.

Mario's Pasta Inns, Inc.
803 King Ave. • Odessa, TX 76514

September 8, 20XX

The Honorable Hank Schlesselman
Representative
Government Offices
9900 Ralston Way
Austin, TX 78603

Dear Mr. Schlesselman:

I am most concerned about your support for H.R. 376. Its stringent restaurant sanitation requirements will double our costs, which will, of course, be passed on to the customer. This may put many restaurants out of business.

Statement of Concern

I own Mario's Pasta Inns, Inc., a chain of 15 Italian restaurants throughout Texas. Additionally, I am the past spokesperson for Restaurateurs International and am an active member of its governing board. Our organization has thoroughly researched sanitation laws for restaurants throughout the world. Texas currently has the most stringent laws and is recognized as a leader in the area of sanitation for restaurants. H.R. 376 in all cases has standards that even our medical labs would have trouble meeting.

Elaboration (optional)

I hope you will seriously consider the impact H.R. 376 would have on our economy. Such a bill can only cause the loss of jobs and income and create disgruntled customers. Please withdraw your support of H.R. 376.

Restate Concern

Sincerely yours,

Signature

Mario Napoli
President

MDN:klu

7

Checklist

- Did you state the purpose of the letter in the first part?
- Did you explain the purpose with details and background information in the second part of the letter?
- Did you summarize the purpose of the letter in the last part?
- Did you use a clear, informative tone?
- If the letter is one of appreciation or thanks, did you use a sincere tone?
- Did you personalize the letter to avoid a form-letter style?

CHAPTER 8

Personal Business Letters

There are times when you write on behalf of yourself rather than for the entire company. This chapter includes samples to help you write personal business letters. The broad categories are as follows:

- Congratulations
- Birthday Wishes
- Holiday Greetings
- Birth of a Child
- Marriage
- Illness — Hospital
- Thank You
- Apology
- Inquiry
- Request
- Refusal

At the side of the page, you will find a brief explanation of each part of the letter. The first letter identifies each section of the letter. Subsequent letters identify only changes to the basic format.

Step-by-Step Guide

These letters are similar to goodwill letters. They are letters in which you promote goodwill toward your employees, their relatives and business associates.

Step 1: The first part of the letter states your purpose. Depending on the reason for writing the letter, this may vary from congratulating a business associate or employee to extending a holiday greeting.

Step 2: The second part of the letter gives the details or background information for the first part. This may include details about an employee's accomplishments or personal comments concerning the first part.

Step 3: The last part of the letter acts as a summary, reminding the recipient of the general nature of the letter. It may include deadlines, a thank-you note or a re-request. It is not necessary in many of the personal business letters to have a third part.

Note: At the end of this chapter is a checklist to use when you write a personal business letter.

Points to Remember Regarding Personal Business Letters

Social-oriented business letters are an excellent way to establish or reinforce relationships in business. The use of personal notes to express thanks, recognition or condolence is considered by many to be a dying art. While fewer and fewer people write these types of notes, almost everyone enjoys receiving them, and these kinds of letters leave a lasting impression.

It is preferable to handwrite personal business notes, although typewritten notes are acceptable. Unless your penmanship is illegible, always try to send a handwritten note in social situations. Keep personal business correspondence short and to the point. Write with sincerity. Do not use business paper for personal notes without company permission. Short notes tend to get lost on a large sheet of paper, so consider notecards or personal stationery for this occasion. Many professionals keep personalized stationery on hand for just such correspondence.

Congratulations

Congratulate an employee, relative of an employee or business associate on an accomplishment.

W & C	*Letterhead*
August 13, 20XX	*Date*
Dear Tim:	*Salutation*
Congratulations on your win in the Junior Division at the Tulsa Rodeo.	*Congratulations*
To be able to win at such a young age is quite an accomplishment. I understand that not only did you win the Junior Division hands-down, but you also came within points of the Senior Division winner.	*Personal Comments (optional)*
Your mom is so proud of you. Congratulations once again!	*Second Congratulations (optional)*
Sincerely,	*Complimentary Close*
Signature	*Signature*
Karen	*Typed Name*
Karen R. Detweiler President, Wilson and Company 1515 W. 23rd Avenue Tulsa, OK 74103	*Additional Information*

8

Congratulations — Social

This letter congratulates an employee, relative of an employee or friend of the company.

Linder Airplanes

August 6, 20XX

Dear Tommy:

Congratulations on winning the soap box derby during My Waterloo Days. Your father couldn't stop talking about how proud he was of your victory.

First Congratulations

I was interested in your win because I, too, was a soap box derby winner 21 years ago in Akron, Ohio. There's nothing quite like the thrill of knowing that something you've made is capable of winning.

Personal Comments (optional)

Congratulations once again and good luck at the Nationals!

Second Congratulations (optional)

Sincerely,

Signature

Charles

Charles M. Norris
President

CMN:cro

Birthday Wishes

This brief letter wishes someone (employee, relative of an employee, friend of the company, business associate) a happy birthday.

May 25, 20XX

Gerri Montgomery
774 Rising Hill Rd.
Lakeland, FL 32340

Dear Gerri:

It's your birthday again! Where has the time gone? We hope your birthday is a happy one. We appreciate your work here at Oglethorpe's and Osman and hope that we enjoy many more birthdays together.

Sincerely,

Signature

Larry

Lawrence Oglethorpe
President, Oglethorpe's and Osman

Birthday Wishes

Holiday Greetings

This short letter wishes an employee or business associate holiday greetings. This is particularly useful for those employees or business associates whose religion is not covered by the standard business greeting cards.

December 15, 20XX

Jenny Schwartz
38 Fairview Ct.
Teasdale, WV 26656

Dear Jenny:

The warmest of holiday greetings to you and your family. We at Gibralter Gems hope this holiday season brings you the best of everything. Our regards to all of you.

Sincerely,

Signature

Tip

Thomas "Tip" Gibralter
Gibralter Gems

Goodwill Greeting

Birth of a Child

This letter congratulates the recipient on the birth of a child.

June 4, 20XX

Dear Lorraine:

There is nothing more exciting than a new baby. You and T.K. must be proud. We were all thrilled to hear about Travis' birth.

First Congratulations

All of us are looking forward to seeing you, T.K. and Travis when you come to visit us next week. That's the time for our traditional "Shower of Gifts."

General Statement

Congratulations, Lorraine! We're all envious of your new little one. Take care of all three of you.

Second Congratulations (optional) Goodwill

Sincerely,

Signature

Shelli

Shelli McAdam
Office Manager
China Dolls for You

8

Marriage

This letter extends congratulations or best wishes when an employee or business associate gets married.

February 22, 20XX

Dear Linda:

On behalf of Smith, Jones and Yanacek, I would like to extend our best wishes on your marriage to Terry Gleason. We all wish you the happiest of times.

First Congratulations

It is always a pleasure to share in the happiness of one of our employees. In your case, it was even more so because you have been such an important part of our firm. I know I speak for all of us when I say that it couldn't have happened to a nicer person. We all look forward to your return after your honeymoon and hope that we will meet Terry soon.

Personal Comment

Best wishes once again. We'll see you in a couple of weeks.

Second Congratulations (optional)

Sincerely,

Signature

Monty

Montgomery Smith
Senior Partner
Smith, Jones and Yanacek
Counselors at Law
231 1st St. S.E.
Remington, MO 63302

8

Illness — Hospital

This letter offers sympathy for an employee who is hospitalized.

January 10, 20XX

Dear Carrie:

I am sorry to hear that you have been hospitalized. I'm sure that the staff at Trinity General will take good care of you and get you on your way. Please call us if you have any questions regarding the company's health insurance.

Sympathy
Goodwill
Assistance

Ft. Dodge Furnaces relies heavily on its employees and will feel your absence. I hope that you will recover quickly. We look forward to your return.

Additional Comments

Sincerely,

Signature

Ole

Ole Munson
President
Ft. Dodge Furnaces

8

Thank You

This letter thanks someone (employee, relative of an employee, business associate) for something that was done.

Wobbly Horse Gift Shop
4866 Kilimanjaro Dr. • Ann Arbor, MI 48897

April 3, 20XX

Dear Mr. Wu:

I want to thank you for sending me the address and phone number of the gift shop in Hong Kong.

First Thank You

I called them this evening to ask about the tablecloths you told me about. You were right. They were most cordial and reasonable in their prices. I was able to order 10 tablecloths at a fraction of what they would have cost here in the States.

Explanation (optional)

Thank you once again for your kind gesture.

Second Thank You

Sincerely,

Signature

Jan Robinson

Apology

This is a formal apology. Such letters usually deal with social events.

Trundle, Trundle and Smith
P.O. Box 2290 • Frost, AZ 85603

December 1, 20XX

Dear Mr. and Mrs. Lambertson:

Please accept my apologies for missing your Thanksgiving brunch on November 23. I hope my last-minute change of plans did not inconvenience you too much.

First Apology

As you know, I had planned on attending and was looking forward to it. However, my brother who lives in Boston, Georgia, had emergency bypass surgery, and his wife asked me to be with her. Had that not happened, naturally I would have been with you.

Explanation and Personal Comments (optional)

Once again, I ask for your understanding in this matter and hope that my frantic, last-minute call to bow out was acceptable.

Second Apology (optional)

Sincerely,

Signature

Thomas J. Trundle, Sr.

8

Inquiry

This letter asks for information to be used by the company.

Cat Man Dew Pet Suppliers
853 Regal Ave. • Oklahoma City, OK 73009

February 14, 20XX

Pekka H. Huovienin
34 Raamintinuu
58 Helsinki 00580
Finland

Dear Mr. Huovienin:

We are trying to locate information on a breed of cat called the Suomi shorthair and understand that you are the leading expert on cats in Finland.

Inquiry
Compliment

We have a client who is interested in buying a Suomi shorthair. She had seen one once at the New York Feline Show but has been unable to locate one since. She came to our shop and requested that we help her. Since the breed originated in Finland, we thought you might be able to give us some more information. We are most interested in the names of breeders that may have kittens for sale.

Explanation

We will call you within the next month to follow up on this inquiry. Thank you for all your trouble. We look forward to talking to you.

Contact Information
Thank You

Sincerely,

Signature

Kathleen "Cat" Pence

KMP:nip

Request

This letter asks an individual or company to act on a request.

8

PDQ Truckers
P.O. Box 2068 • Denver, CO 80393-2068

August 21, 20XX

Cameron Mrstik
Mrstik's Mobile Station
582 Robinwood
Minihaha, MN 55437

Dear Mr. Mrstik:

Would you please return the black leather jacket that was left in your gas station last Saturday?

One of our truckers, Sam MacIntyre, left his leather jacket when he was on a run for us. Another of our truckers mentioned to Sam that he thought he saw a jacket just like Sam's hanging on your wall. He said it had to be Sam's; there are few leather jackets that say, "Ivydale, West Virginia" on them. Sam asked us to call you as he's on vacation in the Bahamas. We have tried repeatedly to reach you by phone, but your phone is always busy.

Please send the jacket as soon as possible, C.O.D. Thank you for your prompt response.

Sincerely,

Signature

Patrick D. Quentin
President

PDQ:msq

	Request
	Explanation
	Specific Information
	Thank You

Refusal

This letter is an answer to the request letter and gives the reasons why the recipient won't act on the writer's request.

Mrstik's Mobile Station
582 Robinwood • Minihaha, MN 55437

August 25, 20XX

Patrick D. Quentin, President
PDQ Truckers
P.O. Box 2068
Denver, CO 80393-2068

Dear Mr. Quentin:

I would like to return Mr. MacIntyre's jacket to him, but I don't have it.   *Refusal*

The jacket your trucker saw says, "I love Dale, Wes and Virginia." I had that jacket made specially for my wife. Those are our three children's names. I checked our register of truckers, and there was no Sam MacIntyre at our station on the Saturday you mentioned. Perhaps he was at Mrs. Rick's Mobile Station on the interstate. The phone number there is 612-555-3827. People get us mixed up all the time.   *Explanation*

                                                                                Added Service

I'm sorry I couldn't help you. I hope Mr. MacIntyre finds his jacket soon.   *Regret*
                                                                                Goodwill

Sincerely,

Signature

Cameron Mrstik

CJM:mjm

Checklist

- Is the tone of the letter sincere?
- Did you state the purpose of the letter in the first part?
- Did you give background information or details in the second part?
- If you used a third part, did you recongratulate, thank or set deadlines for your request?

8

*C*HAPTER 9

Letters of Condolence

Here are samples to help you write the most difficult of all letters to compose: condolence letters. The broad categories are as follows:

- On the Death of a Business Associate
- On the Death of a Mother
- On the Death of a Father
- On the Death of a Wife
- On the Death of a Husband
- On the Death of a Child
- On the Death of a Brother
- On the Death of a Sister

At the side of the page, you will find a brief explanation of each part of the letter. The first letter identifies each section of the letter. Subsequent letters identify only changes to the basic format.

Step-by-Step Guide

Although sympathy cards are available, a letter of condolence is more personal. Letters of condolence should be written with a sincere tone. If at all possible, reflect on the person who has died.

Step 1: The first part of the letter offers your condolences.

Step 2: The second part of the letter, if possible, should reflect on the person who has died. If you knew the person well, personal recollections are appropriate. If you did not know the person well or at all, this part is optional; although, if you can relate this person's life to your own in some way, you should include this part.

Step 3: The last part of the letter offers further condolences or support.

Note: At the end of this chapter is a checklist to use when you write a condolence letter.

Remember

Condolence letters should always be handwritten. It is in very poor taste to type a letter of condolence.

On the Death of a Business Associate

Graham's 573 Westdale Road • Santa Fe, NM 87505	*Letterhead*
October 6, 20XX	*Date*
Dear Lou:	*Salutation*
I was shocked to hear of the death of your partner, Max Wassermann. Although I knew he was ill, I was still taken by surprise by his sudden passing.	*Condolences*
Max and I worked together at the old Cramer's Store in downtown Santa Fe when we first arrived here in 1954. I will never forget his immense capacity for helping other people. I share your sorrow at this time.	*Personal Recollection of Deceased*
If there is any way that I can help, please let me know. Rest assured that your loss is all of Santa Fe's loss.	*Further Condolences or Offers of Support*
Sincerely,	*Complimentary Close*
Geo. "Pinky" Graham	*Signature*

9

On the Death of a Mother

Trains Unlimited

December 11, 20XX

Dear Marilyn:

Please let me extend my deepest sympathy on behalf of all the staff here at Trains Unlimited on the passing of your mother.

Condolences

I know that you spoke many times of how difficult your mother's battle with cancer was. Though we are saddened by her death, I'm sure that we share your relief that she is now at peace. She was a brave woman.

Personal Recollection of Deceased (optional)

Please accept our sympathy. We have taken up a collection for a memorial contribution and have sent it to the American Cancer Society in your mother's name.

Further Condolences or Offers of Support

Sincerely,

Gloria Williams
Vice President, Sales

On the Death of a Father

Lindlemeier's Tree Farms
R.R. 2 • Marlboro, VT 00192

November 1, 20XX

Dear Truk:

We were saddened to hear that your father died last Friday and wish to extend our sympathy.

Condolences

Although we did not know your father well, we did have a chance to meet him on a couple of occasions. He was proud of his new country and of being able to help his children become established here in the United States. Though his loss is painful, you have much to be proud of with your father.

Personal Recollection of Deceased (optional)

If there is some way that Tilly and I can help you and your family, let us know. Please take as much time from work as you need to get your father's affairs in order.

Further Condolences or Offers of Support

Sincerely,

Jake and Tilly Lindlemeier

9

On the Death of a Wife

March 1, 20XX

Dear Charles:

Please accept our condolences on the untimely passing of
your wife, Lydia. It is difficult to understand why such
tragedies happen, and I do not understand why Lydia was
taken from you so early in your life together.

I hope you will now surround yourself with good friends and
the pleasant memories you have of Lydia. I remember her
beaming smile at the company picnics. She seemed to have a
zest for life that few of us do and was willing to share that
zest with others. I shall never forget her enthusiastic win of
the sack race last year.

Please accept what little comfort these words can give you.
If we can help you in any way, please call.

Sincerely,

N.K. Berryhill

Condolences

*Personal Recollection
of Deceased (optional)*

*Further Condolences
Offers of Support*

9

On the Death of a Husband

July 17, 20XX

Dear Mrs. Trotter:

Our deepest sympathy to you and your family on the death of your husband, Ned. He was a dear friend to so many of us here at Thompson's.

Condolences

When Ned first came to Thompson's, he told us that he was here to stay, and stay he did — 35 years. I am happy that he enjoyed a few years of his retirement before he became ill.

Personal Recollection of Deceased (optional)

We at Thompson's are here when you need us. Please accept this token as a memorial for Ned.

Further Condolences Offers of Support

Sincerely,

George Ray Thompson

9

On the Death of a Child

February 23, 20XX

Dear Mr. and Mrs. Nelson:

I was shocked to hear of the death of your son, Bobby. Such losses defy understanding. *Condolences*

Bobby used to come in on Saturday with Ike to the station and listen to me do my show. He was forever wanting me to play John Denver's "Rocky Mountain High." He said it made him feel good. I'll dedicate it to him this Saturday. *Personal Recollection of Deceased (optional)*

If I can do anything to help, call. Ike, I'll cover for you as long as you need. God bless. *Further Condolences Offers of Support*

Sincerely,

Rocky Hopkins

On the Death of a Brother

May 12, 20XX

Dear Ken:

I would like to offer my sympathy to you and your family on the passing of your brother.

Condolences

Although I never met him, I feel as if I knew him from all you've said about him at work. I'm sure his wife and children are pleased to know that you spoke so highly of him and his work with special-needs children. It is a shame that one so gifted must succumb so early in life.

Personal Recollection of Deceased (optional)

If you need someone to talk to when you come back, I'll be here.

Further Condolences Offers of Support

Sincerely,

Wanda Ferguson
Divisional Manager, TeleMarketing

9

On the Death of a Sister

January 4, 20XX

Dear Ron:

I am most sorry to hear that your sister passed away from kidney failure last week.

Condolences

Linda Jean was a joy to work with the two years she was here at Modern Health. She always had such outrageous stories to tell. You can be thankful that she enjoyed life while she was with us.

Personal Recollection of Deceased (optional)

Please offer my sympathy to your family, especially your mother. I'll take care of your mail while you are gone.

Further Condolences Offers of Support

Sincerely,

Terry Glandon
Vice President, Claims

9

Checklist

- Is the letter sincere?
- Does the first part of the letter offer condolences?
- Does the second part of the letter include personal recollections if you knew the deceased?
- Does the third part of the letter offer further condolences and support?
- Does the letter comfort the bereaved?

9

C *HAPTER 10*

Letters About Employment Changes

One of the most demanding writing tasks is searching for a new position or hiring a new employee. Those are the two main categories of this chapter. Topics include the following:

- Reference Request
- Waiver of Confidentiality
- Request for Meeting
- Job Hunter Seeking an Interview
- Interview Confirmation
- Thanks for Interview
- Unsolicited Application
- Cover Letters for Resumés
- Requesting Appointment
- Reply to Unsolicited Application
- Job Application
- Job Hunter Seeking Job With Contact
- Solicited Application
- Job Acceptance
- Job Rejection
- Not Accepting Possible Job Offer

- Positive Resignation
- Negative Resignation
- Response to Job Offer: Covers Terms

Topics also include the following employer responses:

- Request for Employment Reference
- Reference for Former Employee
- Letters of Introduction
- Letter of Recommendation
- Character Reference
- Progress Report
- Rejection of Application
- Response to Rejected Job Application
- Follow-Up After Not Getting the Job
- Rejection of an In-House Job Applicant
- Rejection of an Unsolicited Application
- Rejection of a Solicited Application
- Invitation for an Interview
- Job Offers
- New Employee
- Promotions
- Acceptance of Resignation
- Recommending a Raise

General business letters:

- Rejection of Unsolicited Business
- Request for Material
- Request for Information
- Confirmation to Speaker
- Giving Information
- Discontinuing a Business Relationship
- Rejecting a Request

- Introducing a New Employee

At the side of the page you will find a brief explanation of each part of the letter. The first letter identifies each section of the letter. Subsequent letters identify only changes to the basic format.

Step-by-Step Guide

Letters hiring employees are used by many companies in lieu of a contract drawn up by an attorney and are recognized as legal documents in many courts of law. It is therefore extremely important that you specify each aspect of employment for the prospective employee. Letters in this section also include samples of rejection letters and letters requesting confidential information.

Step 1: The first part of the letter states your purpose. This may be anything from offering a position to requesting information.

Step 2: The second part of the letter gives the details or background information for the first part. If you are offering a position, it is appropriate in this section to give all of the details concerning the position. If you are requesting information, you should explain why you need the information. If you are rejecting an application, you should provide a reason for the rejection. If you are recommending or providing a reference for someone, state specific knowledge, skills and abilities the person has that will benefit the reader.

Step 3: The last part of the letter acts as a summary reminding the recipient of the general nature of the letter. This part clarifies the action that must be taken, if any.

Note: At the end of this chapter is a checklist to use when you write letters to hire employees.

10

Reference Request

Asking a person to be a reference is awkward for most people. This letter will help with that task.

December 2, 20XX | *Date*

Jason Tompkins, Jr. | *Inside Address*
JJT: Heavy Equipment
1288 E. U.S. 63
Sioux City, IA 50585

Dear Jason: | *Salutation*

May I use your name as a reference for a job I hope to get? I am | *Request*
applying for risk manager openings at Johns Oil Company, Fast
Food Inc., and Ploish Publishing. Our experience together at JJT | *Details*
helped give me the confidence to try for these jobs.

Since I graduated with an associate degree in risk management last
spring, I have taken several courses in industrial engineering. I am | *Update*
experienced with OSHA regulations and a variety of plant
operational systems.

Being both co-workers and friends for many years, I naturally
thought of you as a reference. If you are comfortable with that | *Personal Note*
idea, please return the enclosed self-addressed, stamped postcard to
me stating your approval. I'd appreciate your help, of course, but
also understand not wanting strangers calling and wanting inside
information about someone who out-fishes you on every camping
trip. Yet, I know I could have a great career with any of these
companies and could then afford to treat you to a fish dinner at a
fine restaurant!

Thanks either way for being a friend — and the son of a heavy
equipment company owner who hired a poor fisherman years
back! | *Thank You*

Sincerely, | *Complimentary Close*

Signature | *Signature*

Cody | *Typed Name*

10

Waiver of Confidentiality

This letter is a form signed by an employee giving the employer permission to provide information to parties such as welfare agencies or spouses who request it. This protects the employer from a lawsuit for invasion of privacy.

Wholesome Eggs, Inc.
R.R. 3
Bandville, AL 35542

I, the undersigned, acknowledge that my employer has received a request from Crystal Denney for information concerning my employment.

Acknowledgment

I grant my employer full permission to provide the information described as salary history, benefit history and sick leave accrued.

Permission Given

Signature

Lisa Ziesser
Employee

Sept. 5, 20XX

Signature

Typed Name

Date

10

Request for Meeting

Asking for a meeting or an interview is an essential job skill. Here is how to do it.

10

456 El Camino
Santa Fe, NM 87501

April 25, 20XX

Maggie Montoya
Escrow Department
Valley National Bank
P.O. Box 99
Espanola, NM 87532

Dear Ms. Montoya:

Thank you for your response to my April 19, 20XX, inquiry concerning the position of escrow representative at Valley National Bank.

If you have any time available on either May 7 or 8, I would appreciate 10 minutes of your day to review a five-step plan for developing an escrow division in one month. This plan could benefit the entire bank. If the plan interests you, we could then schedule additional time to discuss how I might assist VNB in achieving its escrow goals.

I will call on May 2 to arrange an appointment. I look forward to meeting you in person.

Sincerely,

Signature

Carrie Gonzales

Sender's Address

Thank You
Reference Position

Request

Benefit

Contact Information

Job Hunter Seeking an Interview

This letter uses a request as a "hook" to get into the company. At the same time, the writer is clear in stating her qualifications and desire to be considered in the future for a position.

March 15, 20XX

Mr. Phillip Crenshaw, Personnel Director
ABC Manufacturing
4909 Gen. Bradley NE
Albuquerque, NM 87111

Dear Mr. Crenshaw:

May I have an interview with you to discuss your work in personnel as well as any new directions you see developing in the personnel field?

Request

I am gathering information for an article I am writing on students, graduation, job prospects and future developments in personnel. The article will appear in the local section of *The Kansas City Star*. I would very much like your input for my article.

Reason

I am especially interested in what is taking place in manufacturing companies such as ABC. As a college senior, I will graduate from Kansas University at the end of May with a degree in human resources and business communication. I feel that my education and summer activities, writing news releases for the regional YMCA and developing skill programs for YMCA employees will qualify me in the future for a trainee position in personnel.

Background

I will call your office next Wednesday morning for an appointment time that is convenient. My interview should not take more than 30 minutes.

Contact Information

Sincerely,

Signature

Marion L. Thomas

10

Interview Confirmation

Keeping your name in front of a potential employer is an effective way of persuading someone to hire you. Confirming an interview achieves that purpose while reducing confusion regarding appointment details.

456 El Camino
Santa Fe, NM 87501

May 1, 20XX

Maggie Montoya
Escrow Department
Valley National Bank
P.O. Box 99
Espanola, NM 87532

Dear Ms. Montoya:

Thank you for making time in your schedule to see me on Monday, May 7, at 9:10 a.m.

Thank You

Although I will be brief in my presentation of the five steps to develop an escrow division, I will also be available to address any concerns you may have regarding the achievement of this goal within a month by your escrow staff.

Confirmation

Agenda and Intent

Sincerely,

Signature

Carrie Gonzales

10

Thanks for Interview

Again, keep your name on a potential employer's desk and in her mind. Demonstrating manners is a persuasive tool for obtaining a job, too.

456 El Camino
Santa Fe, NM 87501

May 7, 20XX

Maggie Montoya
Escrow Department
Valley National Bank
P.O. Box 99
Espanola, NM 87532

Dear Ms. Montoya:

Thank you for the interview today. Your joke about the lonesome lawyer still makes me laugh.

Thank You
Reminder

I appreciate your consideration of my qualifications and application for the job of escrow representative. I will check in with you next Monday to see if you have made a decision about the position. If I can answer any questions or concerns, please call me at 555-6678, mornings, if possible.

Contact Information

Thank you again for your interest.

Second Thank You

Sincerely,

Signature

Carrie Gonzales

10

Unsolicited Application

This letter may double as a cover letter for a resumé. The key descriptors are linked directly to the resumé material.

67 No. Hampshire Road
Redmond, WA 98052

October 12, 20XX

Carver, Barrington & Stephens Imports
2345 Brown Ave.
Seattle, WA 98104

Dear Mr. Carver:

I am responding to the in-house posting for the position of associate project manager with your organization. A former colleague, Terry Barrington, alerted me to the opening and suggested that I contact you directly.

I have four years of experience with Michaels & Wade in Redmond, where I specialized in management information systems. As you update your computer network and applications, you will need expertise in every department of your import business. The key descriptors below highlight areas of my experience and education that you will find most pertinent.

Computer skills: DOS, WordPerfect, Lotus, Harvard Graphics; associate's degree in computer science, 1993.

Communication skills: Excellent grammar and usage in writing, good oral presentation and training skills, wrote and delivered annual department report for board of directors.

Sales experience: Retail sales associate as high school and college student for three years at Pier Trading Post.

Supervisory experience: Assistant to the associate warehouse supervisor at Michaels & Wade for four years.

May I arrange a time to meet with you or your agent early next week? I will call your office on Thursday, October 16. I would be available immediately, just in time for the holiday rush at Carver, Barrington & Stephens Imports. My daytime phone number is 555-7889. Please call collect if you have questions.

Sincerely,

Signature

Charlie Lamble

Purpose

Position

Reference

Background

Benefit

Specific Skills

Request

Contact Information
Availability

Cover Letters for Resumés

When faxing a copy of your resumé to a potential employer, also mail or hand deliver a quality copy for the employer's files.

7260 Vista Drive
Denver, CO 80030

March 3, 20XX

Thomas Randolph, Senior Geologist
Gigantic Resources
One Mountain Plaza
Phoenix, Arizona 99065

Dear Tom:

I enjoyed our telephone conversation this morning and was interested to hear about the opening for an exploration geologist at Gigantic Resources. As you requested, I am faxing you a copy of my resumé. I will also be mailing you a copy for your permanent files.

Goodwill

Request
Answer

As I mentioned during our conversation, I am a petroleum geologist with seven years of experience in the Rocky Mountain region. Currently, I am working for Weaver Oil and Gas as their manager of geology. My duties include both prospect generation and sales. I have strong technical abilities and sound written and oral communication skills. Due to family considerations, I am very interested in relocating to the Phoenix area.

Background
(General)

I look forward to meeting with you on April 1. If you wish to contact me before our interview, you may reach me at 303-555-5792.

Contact Information

Thank you again for the information you offered me on the telephone this morning.

Thank You

Sincerely,

Signature

Karl Davis

10

This is an example of a short cover letter for a resumé when there is no knowledge of an available position.

March 14, 20XX

Jane Smith, Personnel
American Academy of Family Physicians
8880 Ward Parkway
Kansas City, Missouri 64114

Dear Ms. Smith:

I am interested in a part-time position with American Academy of Family Physicians as an editor.

Reason

My writing and editing experience include newspaper copy, manuscripts, advertising copy, books, brochures and training manuals.

Background (General)

My resumé is enclosed. If you have questions or need more information, please call me at 555-4866.

Enclosure Contact Information

Sincerely,

Signature

Charles Brenner

Enc.

10

Requesting Appointment

This letter asks for an appointment to discuss future employment. It offers enough information to interest the reader but does not give the detail of a resumé.

604 E. Division Rd.
Terre Haute, IN 47815

March 23, 20XX

Alan Justin, President
Justin and Cramer Publishing
67 West Marcus Street
New York, New York 10032

Dear Mr. Justin:

I am a professional business editor who will be relocating to your area within the next six months. I plan on being in New York City April 22 through April 25. May I have an appointment with you to discuss employment opportunities in the New York City area and specifically with Justin and Cramer Publishing?

Information Request (General)

My expertise is both as an editor and as a business writer. I have six years of experience in business editing: four years as an assistant editor at Smart Company Books and, most recently, two years as a business writing consultant for professional groups. I have also published newsletters for two not-for-profit organizations on a volunteer basis.

Background

If it is convenient, may I schedule time to talk with you between April 22 and 25? I will call your office the week of April 1 to determine if there is a time you will be available. In the meantime, if you have any questions or need additional information, please contact me at 219-555-9846.

Request (Specific)

Contact Information

Sincerely,

Signature

Alice Moses

Reply to Unsolicited Application

This letter answers a job inquiry when there is no opening.

David Smith Advertising
P.O. Box 983
St. Louis, MO 63117

January 5, 20XX

Michael Korslund
7320 Pershing
St. Louis, MO 63130

Dear Mr. Korslund:

Your letter inquiring about employment opportunities in our company was forwarded to me from Personnel because of your interest in advertising and copywriting. I am pleased you thought of David Smith Advertising.

Thank You

At this time, however, all our writing slots are filled, and I do not anticipate there being any openings this year. I will ask Personnel to keep your letter on file for three months. In April, let them know if you still want to be considered for an opening.

Reasons

Negative News
Option

Sincerely,

Signature

Robert S. Wood
Creative Director

Job Application

This letter responds to a job advertisement; it includes the background of the writer and asks for an interview.

5314 Delaware
Kansas City, MO 64133

April 19, 20XX

Janet Armstrong
Taggerty and Sons Publishing
673 South Michigan Ave.
Chicago, IL 60603

Dear Ms. Armstrong:

I am writing in response to your advertisement in the December issue of *Publishers Monthly Journal*, in which you announced an opening for a sales representative with Taggerty and Sons Publishing.

Purpose
Position

I have five years of retail experience in the book industry. For the past three years, I have managed Books for Us, an independent bookstore located in Rolling Hills. I am familiar with the products that you publish and believe my experience as a retailer and with the buying public would benefit your company. As the manager of an independent bookstore, I have demonstrated my ability to set goals and complete projects in a timely and thorough manner.

Reference

Background

In my current job, I am responsible for buying both new publications and backlist inventory as well as analyzing sales trends using a computerized inventory system. I have a B.A. in English literature, and I am an active participant in local writers' workshops. I have enclosed a copy of my resumé for your review.

Specific Skills

Enclosure

I would like to meet with you and will contact your office the week of April 27 to determine if an interview may be arranged. If you wish to contact me before that date, please call
555-2434.

Request
Contact Information

Sincerely,

Signature

Frances Hatcher

Enc.

10

Job Hunter Seeking Job With Contact

This letter asks for a job interview and mentions a contact.

November 10, 20XX

Mr. Robert J. Hunter
Director, Internal Communications
United Telephone, Inc.
P.O. Box 3245
Winston Salem, NC 27106

Dear Mr. Hunter:

John Stewart, your director of public relations, told me that you were looking for a communications specialist. I am a recent graduate of Richmond University and would like the opportunity to talk with you about the position.

My degree is in journalism, and my intern work during my senior year was on the community desk at *The Kansas City Star*. The summer of 20XX, I assisted the editor of the St. Joseph Hospital newsletter and was responsible for writing the articles and taking pictures.

May I have an appointment to discuss my qualifications and my interest in working with you as a communications specialist? I will call your office Wednesday morning for a time that is convenient for you.

Sincerely,

Signature

Joan Eldon Williams

| *Contact* |
| *Reason* |
| *Background* |
| *Request* |
| *Contact Information* |

Solicited Application

Although the employer initiates contact in this situation, the job seeker must respond with a personal sales pitch, such as this sample letter.

77 Longmeadow Ave.
Tulsa, OK 74135

August 3, 20XX

David Fronte, Vice President
Professional Chemical Institute
864 Manhattan
Pittsburg, KS 66762

Dear Mr. Fronte:

Thank you for your telephone call this morning requesting my application for product developer. I am pleased that our friend, Kelly Greene, spoke so highly of me.

Reminder
Position
Reference

Your call came at an opportune time in my career. I am encouraged that your company's direction may be the very avenue I have sought for several new product ideas. Your goal of a 10 percent increase in products during the next two years is a challenge I am ready to accept.

Benefit

I am eager to discuss this potential growth with you next Wednesday in your office at 2:15 p.m., as you suggested in our conversation today. In the meantime, please call me at 316-555-9975 should you need additional information prior to our meeting.

Confirmation

Contact Information

Thank you again for your interest.

Thank You

Sincerely,

Signature

Brad Reed

10

Job Acceptance

Put this in writing! Confirm the specifications as you understand them.

One Tailgate Dr.
Sioux City, IA 50584

December 15, 20XX

Mr. Kevin Johns
Johns Oil Company
R.R. Box 45
Sioux City, IA 50523

Dear Mr. Johns:

It is a pleasure to accept the position of risk manager, effective January 3, 20XX. I am eager to begin my new assignment.

Acceptance
Date

Thank you for your confidence in me. I will do my best to surpass the challenge presented by Johns Oil Company's phenomenal growth.

Thank You
Intent

Sincerely,

Signature

Cody Helm

Job Rejection

This situation is difficult. If you know the job is a mismatch for your skills, be honest and then act to remedy the situation. Your integrity and credibility will expand with this letter.

174 Bittersweet St.
Broken Arrow, OK 74012

January 18, 20XX

Carol Connell, Director
Intercomp, Inc.
P. O. Box 23659
Tulsa, OK 74133

Dear Ms. Connell:

The position of executive drafting assistant sounds exciting. Thank you for considering me. However, I cannot accept this offer in good conscience at this time. — *Position* *Thank You* *Rejection*

The computer expertise this position requires for success demands more experience than I currently have. I want to do an excellent job; therefore, I am enrolling in a CAD course at Tulsa University. In four months I will have the training to pursue a similar position with determination. — *Reason* *Decision*

Perhaps TU instructors can suggest names of recent students who are prepared now to accept the responsibilities of the job. Someone better trained than I is waiting to discover Intercomp. — *Suggestion for Alternative*

Thank you again for thinking of me. It has been the incentive I needed to get the extra training I must have to continue in the drafting field. I intend to be prepared for the next executive drafting assistant opening as your company continues to expand its operation. — *Second Thank You* *Intent*

Sincerely,

Signature

Chris Jensen

10

Not Accepting Possible Job Offer

This letter is positive and suggests a continuing business relationship in the future.

June 23, 20XX

Veronica Black
President
Quinta Exploration
P.O. Box 1312
Phoenix, AZ 85029

Dear Veronica:

Thank you for your letter notifying me that I am one of your final candidates for the position of corporate vice president. I certainly enjoyed meeting with you Tuesday, touring the company and learning more about the goals of your board.

Goodwill

However, as we discussed at our meeting, my priority has been to settle on the East Coast, and I have continued to pursue opportunities. Recently, I received an offer in my field of hydrogeology, located within a day's drive of the coast and in proximity to family members. With the responsibilities that are inherent in the position and the future that it promises, I have accepted the offer.

Reason

Result

I hope that we meet again, perhaps at the national conference next summer. Since it is scheduled for Atlanta, I can promise you a tour of the city.

Future
Goodwill

Thank you again for the fine day at Quinta Exploration.

Thank You

Sincerely,

Signature

Janet T. Lundquist

Positive Resignation

When you must "move on" to accept new opportunities, use this sample to guide the draft of your resignation. It can be very brief, basically providing a formal notice for documentation purposes. Or, it may provide an explanation. Employers appreciate understanding the situation.

34458 Seminole Lane
Tampa, FL 33640

February 2, 20XX

Jerry Sanderstein
Sanderstein Aviation
8865 Hidden River Parkway
Tampa, FL 33637

Dear Jerry:

With deep regret and with some excitement, I must resign as night shift supervisor, effective March 1, 20XX. My family will be relocating to Georgia this spring so my wife can pursue a lucrative offer in a law firm. This is an opportunity we cannot overlook.

Feelings
Resignation
Date
Reason

I will be glad to assist in the training of my replacement. Our night shift has a couple of competent workers who would make excellent shift supervisors.

Assistance Offer

Your encouragement during the past nine years has allowed me to grow in my responsibilities and capabilities. Thank you for these successful years. I will miss you, Jerry, as well as all my other friends at Sanderstein Aviation. Your leadership provides me with many fond memories. I wish you continued success.

Thank You
Personal Note

Sincerely,

Tom

10

Negative Resignation

When you must leave a position under duress or stress, keep your explanation short, honest and positive. Never write a resignation letter when you're angry. Remember the adage: "Don't burn bridges." The goal is to state any serious conflict calmly, rationally and gracefully. Despite your differences, you may need a reference from this employer in the future.

345 Cedar Lake Road
Minneapolis, MN 55426

July 14, 20XX

Leslie Young, Marketing Director
Marketing Towers
60 S. Ninth St.
Minneapolis, MN 55402

Dear Ms. Young:

I am resigning my position as special accounts representative, effective July 30, 20XX.

Resignation Date

Recent circumstances incompatible with my personal values require that I change my employment.

Reason

Thank you for the chance to work and learn at Marketing Towers.

Thank You

Sincerely,

Signature

Julie Mast

Response to Job Offer: Covers Terms

This letter responds to a job offer. The writer covers the terms of employment in this reply.

1231 Holly Drive
Carrollton, Texas 75007

July 16, 20XX

Edward Harris
Jenkins, Louis & Albright
505 Santa Fe Ave.
Coppell, TX 75019

Dear Mr. Harris:

I am looking forward to beginning my position as office manager at Jenkins, Louis & Albright effective August 1. Thank you for the confidence you have shown in my abilities.

Acceptance
Date
Thank You

In reviewing our conversation regarding my compensation, it is my understanding that the position pays $26,000 per year and that my salary will be reviewed on an annual basis beginning one year after I start with the company. I will receive both medical and dental insurance as stipulated in the health-care enrollment package I was given during my second interview on July 11. In addition, I am entitled to two weeks of paid vacation per year after I have been with the company 12 months. I recognize that I must schedule my vacation at least four weeks in advance and arrange for a temporary replacement to fulfill my duties while I am away.

Terms

I am pleased to be associated with Jenkins, Louis & Albright.

Compliment

Sincerely,

Signature

Melissa Waters

10

Request for Employment Reference

This letter is from a company requesting a reference from a job applicant's previous employer.

TicToc Clocks, Inc.
8071 Speedway • Indianapolis, IN 46107

February 28, 20XX

J. Carson Jamison, President
Weatherman Time
33 Little House Road
Columbus, OH 43230

Dear Mr. Jamison:

We recently received an application from Carl Olson for the position of master carpenter with our firm. We understand he was previously employed by you.

Statement of Candidate

We would appreciate any information you could give us concerning Mr. Olson's work habits, expertise as master carpenter and attitude. We would also appreciate you sharing with us the reason he no longer works for your firm.

Explanation of Request

We look forward to hearing from you in early March. Please advise us if the information you provide is confidential. Thank you for your time in answering this request.

Deadline

Thank You

Sincerely,

Signature

James Vries
President

JBV:llo

Reference for Former Employee

This letter is a reference for a former employee who is seeking employment elsewhere.

Grant Middle School
901 Third St. • Columbia, OH 43230

March 12, 20XX

Wendell R. Rathbourne, Principal
Jasper Heights Middle School
444 Calbryne Road
Shaker Heights, OH 44139

Dear Mr. Rathbourne:

Pauline O'Malley was employed as a teacher associate at Grant Middle School from April 1988 to June 1988. She was terminated because of a decrease in funding for special education.

Statement of Previous Employment

During Ms. O'Malley's brief tenure, she performed her duties very well. She was a teacher associate for eighth-grade behavioral-disorders classes and was well-liked by both students and staff. The teachers she worked with speak highly of her abilities and willingness to cooperate.

Explanation of Performance

I recommend Ms. O'Malley for any teacher associate position. Please feel free to call me or Marian Thompson, her past supervisor, for further information.

Recommendation Contact Information

Sincerely,

Signature

Lillian M. Detterding
Principal

LMD:gan

159

Letters of Recommendation

This letter recommends a former employee who has requested the reference.

Hirsch & Hirsch
Attorneys at Law
1005 Grand Avenue, Suite 300
Kansas City, Missouri 64106

March 13, 20XX

Mr. Kevin Doerter, City Manager
City of Burlington
P.O. Box 490
Burlington, KS 66839

Dear Mr. Doerter:

Elizabeth Kidder, who has applied for the position of city clerk/finance director for the city of Burlington, has asked me to provide you with a letter of recommendation. I am pleased to comply with her request.

Reason

Ms. Kidder was the personnel clerk at the City of Olathe, Olathe, Kansas, when I began as personnel director in September 20XX. I found her to be very capable.

Previous Employment

During the two years that she reported to me, Ms. Kidder was extremely skilled in handling the administration of all office functions, which included supervising the part-time clerk.

Explanation of Performance

Ms. Kidder is a self-starter, a capable and efficient supervisor, and an exceptional worker. I give Ms. Kidder my highest recommendation. She would be a valuable member of your team.

Recommendation

Sincerely,

Signature

James W. Davis
Partner

JWD:the

Letters of recommendation emphasize how a person worked on a previous job and her expertise. They should also include the relationship between the one seeking the job and the person writing the recommendation, and the length of the acquaintance. Don't hesitate to be enthusiastic, but be sure the candidate can live up to your comments.

10

GRANT WOOD HIGH SCHOOL
319 30th St. S.E. • Cedar Rapids, IA 52403

January 16, 20XX

Linda A. Hagerman, Principal
Thomas Jefferson High School
788 Muscatine Ave.
Iowa City, IA 52240

Dear Ms. Hagerman:

It is with great pleasure that I recommend Mary Alice Westerly for the physics position at Thomas Jefferson.

Introduction

Mrs. Westerly taught at Grant Wood High School from 1978 to 1986, during which time I was principal. Her primary teaching responsibilities were physics, chemistry and ninth-grade general science. She was one of the best teachers we have ever had in the area of science, and we were deeply saddened when she and her family moved to Augusta, Maine. I can assure you that if I had a teaching position open in science, I would hire her. She is creative, deeply conscientious, professional and hard-working.

Relationship to the Writer

Background Information

Attributes of Person Recommended

I strongly recommend her and am sure you will be more than satisfied with her performance in the classroom.

Recommendation

Sincerely,

Signature

Tom Maxwell
Principal

TJM:mer

Character Reference

Similar to the letter of recommendation, the character reference refers only to the character of the person. You should include your relationship with the person and how long you have known her.

St. John's-by-the-Lake Episcopal Church
298 Lakeshore Drive • Brandenburg, MN 56315

May 29, 20XX

Klosterman Employment Agency
22 Linden Blvd.
Brandenburg, MN 56315

Dear Sir or Madam:

I am most pleased to write a character reference for JoAnn Osterson.

Introduction

I have known JoAnn since I first moved to Brandenburg, when she was 3 years old. As rector of St. John's-by-the-Lake Episcopal Church, I have been able to watch JoAnn mature into the fine young lady she is today. She is a tireless worker, having given the most volunteer hours of any of our young adults in the parish. She is always cheerful and dependable.

Relationship to the Writer
Background Information

Attributes of Person
Recommended

I am sure that whoever hires her will find her to be a good worker as well as a pleasant person. She is truly a gem.

Recommendation

Sincerely,

Signature

Louis R. Stanley
Rector

LRS:kpw

Letter of Introduction

This letter introduces a person to a company or individual. Letters of introduction are similar to references, quite often describing the qualifications of the person to be introduced.

10

Campbell, Wilson and Sons
472 Captain's Drive • Boston, MA 02031

October 7, 20XX

R. H. Wing
333 B. Ave., E.
Lincoln, NE 68530

Dear R.H.:

I would like to introduce James N. Glandorf, who will be moving to Lincoln in November. As a fellow Pi Kappa Kappa, would you consider him for a position with your firm?

Introduction
Request

Mr. Glandorf worked in our law office during this last year. He was given the assignment of divorce cases, which he handled extremely well, and was well on his way to establishing himself as one of the best divorce lawyers I have ever seen. James was in line for a partnership here also but wanted to return to his native Nebraska, which I understand, being a Midwesterner myself. I have enclosed a reference from each of our partners. I'm sure you'll find that all of us held James in the highest regard.

Background of Person
Introduced and
Relationship to the
Writer

Please take time to read the references, and extend our greetings to James when he arrives. I have promised him nothing but am sure that you will help him in any way that you would any other fellow Pi Kappa Kappa.

Request

Clarification

Sincerely,

Signature

George R. Campbell
Senior Partner

GRC:lpw
Enc. (4)

Progress Report

An evaluation or progress report is an essential communication for anyone's career. Keep an honest, positive tone that focuses on specifics.

10

August 30, 20XX

Chairperson
Academic Professional Development Committee
St. Paul School of Theology
5123 Truman Road
Kansas City, MO 64127

Dear Chairperson:

Recently, the Reverend Kendall Campbell, the registrar and financial aid director at St. Paul, asked Mr. Lee Yoon Park to obtain a summary of progress for his language studies this summer. I am delighted to report to you that he is an exceptional student who would have earned an A in English had he opted for a grade and credit. I was fortunate to be his instructor.

Purpose

Evaluation

Relationship

Mr. Park spent approximately 25 hours of intense conversation and study of written English with me in June and July. This time was significantly dwarfed by the vast hours of self-directed study he completed between each of our meetings. This self-direction shows his determination to overcome any language obstacles he may still experience.

Duration of Relationship

Character

Observations

During our meetings, I was amazed at Mr. Park's insight and humor. His wit is a joy to experience and to learn from. He asks profound questions, such as, "What is your parenting philosophy?" He shares his Korean heritage and history with those of us who ask. He reads sophisticated literature — including some I have not read yet! He travels with his family and friends as often as he has the opportunity, especially making trips to national parks throughout the United States. All of these activities testify to Mr. Park's value of learning. His ability to communicate increases regularly.

Mr. Park's ability to communicate goes far beyond his knowledge of either American English or Korean — his ability touches the center of our mutual humanity. Thank you for recognizing my friend's promise and for supporting his efforts.

Insight

Thank You

Sincerely,

Signature

Bree Biesner, M.A.

Rejection of Application

The only thing worse than writing a rejection letter is receiving one. Everyone who applies for a position deserves common courtesy. Be clear, yet gentle, in your approach. Give the bad news in the opening sentence and then go on to explain the cause. You may want to compliment the applicant.

WEST TELECOMMUNICATIONS
103 Randolph St.
Chicago, IL 60601

July 26, 20XX

Janna Hazelden, Senior Actuary
Waldron Hotels
278 Main Blvd.
El Paso, TX 79902

Dear Ms. Hazelden:

Thank you for giving us the opportunity to review your qualifications for actuary.   *Thank You*

Although we do not currently have an opening in our accounting department, we are always looking for competent people. May we keep your file active during the next 90 days should any possibilities open up? We will notify you immediately if a position becomes available.   *Rejection/Reason*   *Compliment*   *Request*

In the meantime, good luck in your job search. I am sure that with your background you will find a suitable position soon.   *Goodwill*   *Personal Note*

Sincerely,

Signature

Rod Finney
Personnel Director

Responses to Rejected Job Application

This letter is a follow-up to not being hired. It leaves the door open for a call if another opening occurs. The tone of the letter is friendly and professional.

10

2343 South 10th
Eugene, OR 97405

July 21, 20XX

Marcus Edwards, Personnel Director
Tachert & Hood Manufacturing
P.O. Box 8452
Eugene, OR 97405

Dear Mr. Edwards:

Thank you for considering me for the position of account supervisor at Tachert & Hood. I understand that my qualifications are not in line with your company's needs at the present time.

Thank You

I am very impressed with your company. I believe that Tachert & Hood continues to be successful because of the skill of your management in analyzing the direction of market trends. I hope you will consider me again should another employment opportunity compatible with my experience become available.

Goodwill

Request

If you wish to contact me, please call 555-3416.

Contact

Thank you again for the opportunity to interview with Tachert & Hood.

Second Thank You (optional)

Sincerely,

Signature

Joyce Andrews

Follow-Up After Not Getting the Job

This letter is a response to a previous one informing the reader a job has been filled. It is positive and leaves the door open for future contact with the company.

Janet E. Thompkins
2244 West Nassau Street
Aurora, CO 80013

October 21, 20XX

James Smith
Smith Engineering
P.O. Box 2955
Denver, CO 80206

Dear Mr. Smith:

I appreciate your promptness in writing that the director of human resources has been selected. The opportunity to discuss the position and find out about your company was a pleasure, as was meeting the staff. Thank you.

Appreciation

Thank You

If, in the future, a position is open at Smith Engineering that would fit my goals, background and experience, please call me. I am committed to this area and the human resource field and, of course, am very interested in Smith Engineering.

Goodwill

Sincerely,

Signature

Janet E. Thompkins

10

Rejection of an In-House Job Applicant

This letter turns down an employee's request for a new job within the company.

Powell Glove Company
4709 South 110th Street
Omaha, Nebraska 68127

October 10, 20XX

John Holiday
304 Spruce St.
Omaha, NE 68128

Dear John:

Thank you for your interest in becoming part of Powell's training and development department as an instructor. I agree that everyone needs a change once in a while. However, though you have good production experience, this position requires in-depth knowledge of the training process. *Goodwill* / *Agreement*

Although you have been with Powell for five years, your background and experience have not prepared you for this particular position. Several applications have been received from people with training experience and even some with training experience in the manufacturing industry. The company will fill the position from these applicants. *Rejection* / *Reason*

Unfortunately, you are not being selected for this position, but I am aware that you wish to continue to upgrade your position with the company. I encourage you to do this, and I'm sure that we — the company and you — will find the position that best matches your experience and background. *Encouragement*

Again, I appreciate your interest and hard work in the company and wish you luck in all your future promotions. *Goodwill*

Sincerely,

Signature

John Williams
President

JW:gd

Rejection of an Unsolicited Application

This letter is used to inform an applicant that there are no positions available at the present time for which she is qualified.

First National Bank
223 Ames • Casper, WY 82676

August 30, 20XX

Kelly Flanders
1795 Whisper Lane, #3
Casper, WY 82676

Dear Ms. Flanders:

Your qualifications are impressive. Unfortunately, we are not presently hiring bank tellers.

Compliment
Rejection

As you may know, we recently went through a major expansion. However, we have filled all of our bank teller positions and do not foresee any change in staff in the near future. We will, however, keep your application on file for one year should something arise.

Reason for Rejection

Added Service

Thank you for your interest in First National. If you should have any questions, please call me.

Thank You

Sincerely,

Signature

Hiram Scott
Vice President, Human Resources

HMS:ald

10

Rejection of a Solicited Application

This letter is used to inform an applicant that the position for which she applied has been offered to someone else.

10

Morton Engineering
3457 Randall St. N.E. • Armond, AR 72310

January 25, 20XX

K.J. Land
356 Denver
University of Nebraska
Lincoln, NE 68308

Dear Ms. Land:

Thank you for applying at Morton Engineering. I am sorry that we are unable to offer you the position of electrical engineer for which you recently interviewed.

We have selected another person who has the type of experience we feel is necessary for the position. I enjoyed interviewing you and hope that you are successful in your employment search in the near future.

If you should have any questions, please call me.

Sincerely,

Signature

Hanna Westcott
Personnel Director

HJW:kmm

Thank You

Rejection

Reason for Rejection
Goodwill

Contact Information

Invitation for an Interview

Arrange appointment specifications for easy, quick visual access. This letter can set the tone for the actual interview.

HILL MULTI-MEDIA CORPORATION
301 E. Armour Blvd. • Kansas City, MO 64111

March 5, 20XX

Kay E. Anders
7923 Noland Road
Lenexa, KS 66215-2528

Dear Ms. Anders:

Thank you for your application for the position of communications director. We are pleased to invite you to be interviewed for the position. Your interview has been scheduled as follows:

Date:	March 17, 20XX
Time:	11:15 a.m.
Location:	Conference Room A
	Second Floor (Northeast)
	Gillham Plaza Building
	301 E. Armour Blvd.
	Kansas City, MO 64111
Parking:	Underground area off Gillham Road

You can expect to meet with the committee for 30 to 45 minutes. If you have any questions, please contact me at 816-555-6889.

Again, thank you for your interest in the position.

Sincerely,

Signature

Carol J. Kennedy
Interim Director of Programs

CJK:dmc

Acknowledgment

Request

Details

Expectations

Contact Information

Thank You

10

Job Offers

These letters are used to offer a position to a potential employee and should be treated as a legal contract. Be clear that the offer is formal and official. It should outline all of the essential information the potential employee needs to make a decision. It is fine to make the informal offer by telephone and then follow up at once with a formal letter. Be sure to make the potential employee feel welcome.

Morton Engineering
3457 Randall St. N.E. • Armond, AR 72310

January 25, 20XX

J. Wallace Mercer
7898 Talleyho Lane
Lexington, KY 40329

Dear Mr. Mercer:

It is with great pleasure that I am able to offer you a position at Morton Engineering as an electrical engineer.

Job Offer

The position pays $35,000 annually, in equal increments every other Friday. Additionally, you will receive two weeks of paid vacation every 12 months, a bonus equaling two weeks' salary payable the payday before Christmas, health benefits and $25,000 of life insurance. This position is a two-year agreement, after which it may be renegotiated. Either party may terminate with a two-week notice.

Outline the Position

We are very pleased to offer you the position and are sure that you will make a superb addition to our firm. If you have any questions, please call me at any time.

Welcome

Sincerely,

Signature

Hanna Westcott
Personnel Director

HJW:kmm

The specifics of the job offer are enclosed; the letter is upbeat and friendly.

Omega Corporation
P.O. Box 666 • Phoenix, AZ 99065

March 2, 20XX

Jessica Carswell
3498 Grant
Overland Park, KS 66214

Dear Jessica:

I am pleased to offer you the position of public relations director at Omega Corporation. We all appreciate your fine background and experience in the public relations field as well as your interest in building up the public relations department at Omega. Your selection by the committee and board will enhance the fine professional team that sets the direction for Omega Corporation.

I am enclosing in this letter the items we discussed in our last meeting, on February 23: the terms of employment and your benefits as a member of our team. I have also added specific information, brochures, etc., from each of our medical insurance carriers so that you may consider your insurance options.

John, I am personally very pleased that our discussions ended on such a positive note — for both of us. I'll meet you in my office at 8:30 Tuesday morning, March 21, to make sure that you get around to meet everyone.

Sincerely,

Signature

Robert C. Hanks
President

RCH:gk
Enc.

Job Offer

Compliment

Details

Enclosures

Goodwill
Contact Information

10

This letter affirms the reader's employment and the writer's choice of applicants.

Haven Home
P.O. Box 124 • Memphis, TN 38124

September 15, 20XX

Kory Chandler
45 Main Drive
Memphis, TN 38118

Dear Kory:

We are pleased that your experience and education match our needs for a fund-raiser and program coordinator. Your enthusiasm convinced the interview committee that you are the appropriate match for Haven Home.

Job Offer
Compliment

Your vision for adding follow-up questionnaires to our first-time clients is a dynamic idea. That effort will initiate many improvements in our service to family members experiencing domestic violence. At the same time, the questions will increase awareness of personal choices in our clients living with violence.

Contribution

The transition and training schedule for your first week at Haven Home is attached. Please review it for Monday morning at 7:30.

Attachment

If there is anything I can do to help make your transition more comfortable, please let me know. My voice-mail number is 64. I'll check in with you later to see how your first day is going.

Contact Information

Welcome to our team!

Welcome

Sincerely,

Signature

Anna Phelps
Executive Director

AP:dmc

10

New Employee

This letter welcomes a new employee to a business.

Pink's Shears, Inc.
763 Kekke Dr. • Hibbing, MN 21111

May 6, 20XX

Linda Jean Tremel
1205 Mickey Mouse Dr.
Orlando, FL 32078

Dear Ms. Tremel:

It is my distinct pleasure to welcome you to Pink's Shears, Inc. We are looking forward to your arrival on May 21.

First Welcome

We at Pink's are very proud of our complete line of pinking shears and know that you will take the same pride in your work as we do in ours. Your role as sales director will be an important one. We know that your education and experience will bring to Pink's a much-needed momentum.

General Comments

Specific Position

Once again, welcome to Pink's. If there is any way I can help you make the transition, let me know.

Second Welcome

Sincerely,

Signature

Harold "Pinky" Pinkham
President

HJP:cpa

10

Promotion — Congratulations

This letter congratulates an employee or business associate on her promotion.

Cadrell's
290 26th Ave. • Winston, GA 30067

August 8, 20XX

T. Molly Rathburn
8944 Tripp
Winston, GA 30067

Dear Molly:

I would like to congratulate you on your recent promotion to assistant plant supervisor. You must be proud of your accomplishments.

First Congratulations

Because of your hard work and dedication, you deserve this promotion. Employees like you help Cadrell's keep ahead of the competition and lead the way in the field of dental equipment. Your efforts are appreciated.

General Statement (optional)

Congratulations again. Welcome to the management team at Cadrell's.

Second Congratulations

Sincerely yours,

Signature

J.K. Cadrell, Jr.
President

JKC:ltj

Announcing a Promotion — Personal

This letter announces the promotion of an employee.

Nacogdoches Notebooks
277 Linden • Nacogdoches, TX 75963

August 1, 20XX

Truc Phan
3009 Clipclop Lane
Nacogdoches, TX 75963

Dear Mr. Phan:

We are pleased to offer you the promotion to vice president in charge of sales.

Announcement

Nacogdoches Notebooks is promoting you because of your outstanding and untiring commitment to your work. Nacogdoches Notebooks has grown substantially because of your efforts.

Reason

Please see Ray Norton on Monday. He will show you your new office and begin your orientation.

Instructions

Congratulations. We are proud to have you associated with our company.

Congratulations

Sincerely,

Signature

Susanna M. Graham
President

SMG:eer

10

Announcing a Promotion — Internal

This memo announces the promotion of an employee to other members of the firm. In certain circumstances a letter may be used, also.

MEMORANDUM

Date: August 5, 20XX
To: All Employees
From: Susanna Graham, President
Re: Promotion to Vice President/Sales

We are pleased to announce the promotion of Truc Phan to vice president in charge of sales.

Announcement

In the past 12 months, Mr. Phan has consistently provided outstanding service to his clients, brought in several new accounts and demonstrated outstanding sales leadership. Nacogdoches Notebooks has grown substantially because of Mr. Phan's work. He will assume his new position on August 10 and will be located in Suite 25.

Reason

Please join me in congratulating Mr. Phan on his new position.

Congratulations

Acceptance of Resignation

Always accept a resignation with dignity. Allow the letter to reflect your personal investment in the relationship. This letter shows that a friendship exists. If that is not your situation, omit the personal comments.

Merl Garrett, Supervisor of Nurses
University Medical Center
5000 University Parkway
Laguna Heights, CA 92677

May 12, 20XX

Sherri Lu, Senior Floor Nurse
University Medical Center
5020 University Parkway
Laguna Heights, CA 92677

Dear Sherri:

We regret you must leave and reluctantly accept your resignation as senior floor nurse beginning June 1, 20XX. We do, however, understand that personal medical concerns demand your attention now.

Regret
Acceptance
Reason

Your contributions to University Medical Center will remain after your departure: better documentation, better patient service and improved staff morale. Thank you for your hard work in every aspect of your job. Your dedication to us shows in your willingness to help train your replacement. We have always been able to count on you.

Contributions

Thank You

We wish you the best of health. I will miss you immensely. Please stay in touch.

Goodwill
Personal Note

Sincerely,

Signature

Merl

10

179

Recommending a Raise

This letter recommends giving a raise before the first year's anniversary. It includes the reasons supporting the request.

Aaron Computer Mapping
1472 Marquette Avenue
Montgomery, AL 36044

October 5, 20XX

William Aaron, President
Aaron Computer Mapping
1472 Marquette Avenue
Montgomery, AL 36044

Dear Bill:

I recommend that we offer Matthew Martin, a draftsman in our city planning section, a raise of $1,500 per year effective November 1. This would bring his annual salary up to $19,500.

I am highly satisfied with the quality of work he produces and his commitment to Aaron Computer Mapping. He is a very conscientious employee, finishing tasks in an accurate and timely manner. He is aware of our reputation of excellence in the computer mapping field and maintains that degree of excellence in his work.

Although Matthew has been with our company only six months, I am recommending that his salary be increased and that his annual salary review take place one year from this month. He has been a great asset to Aaron Computer Mapping and should be rewarded for his outstanding work.

Sincerely,

Signature

Pat Norris

Recommendation

Reasons (specific)

Recommendation

Reason

Rejection of Unsolicited Business

This letter withdraws quotes that have already been given.

MERION INSURANCE
7542 Warner Place
Chicago, IL 60603

May 10, 20XX

Lisa Reiters
Managed Care Insurance Marketing Corporation
P.O. Box 1051
Los Angeles, CA 90052

RE: 1933 Sterling Silverware

Dear Lisa:

As we discussed today, Merion is withdrawing the quotes that I sent you on this case. In reviewing the information that was supplied, we don't feel this would be a good risk for Merion.

Statement of Reason

I'm sorry this couldn't be a more favorable response, but I look forward to working with you at another time.

Goodwill

Sincerely,

Signature

Joyce Cole
Supervisor

JC/mj

Request for Material

In giving instructions, this letter states clearly what is needed — as well as what is not needed.

James Insurance
P.O. Box 245 • Eugene, OR 97405

March 16, 20XX

Robert James
P.O. Box 9822
Des Moines, IA 50306-9822

Dear Robert:

This is to confirm our telephone conversation regarding claims reporting and updating. As I indicated on Wednesday, I am receiving too much paper from you. I do not want hospital records, doctors' handwritten notes or copies of pleadings other than the complaint.

Reason

I do need the following:

Instructions

1. A completed first report
2. Your report of claim
3. Defense counsel's initial analysis of liability and quantum
4. The most current narrative medical report that best describes the claimant's history, diagnosis and prognosis

Also, if the defense counsel's assessment of the case changes, I must have notification of that as well.

If I need other information, the burden will be on me to request it. I hope this letter will serve to clarify exactly what I need regarding insurance reporting.

Goodwill

Thank you for your cooperation.

Sincerely,

Signature

George L. Sherman, J.D.
Assistant Secretary

GLS:db

Request for Information

This letter requests information.

Rinehart Consulting Engineers
San Jose, CA 95117

May 10, 20XX

Mr. Richard Webly
Lodge of the Good Seasons
611 South Michigan
Chicago, IL 60603

Dear Mr. Webly:

Rinehart Consulting is interested in holding its annual team-building staff meeting in Chicago the weekend of October 10, 20XX.

Reason

We are planning on attendance of 12 staff members who would arrive in time for dinner on Friday, October 9. We need a breakfast buffet for Saturday and Sunday, October 10 and 11, and a buffet lunch and sit-down dinner on Saturday. Twenty-five people will be at each meal. The meeting room for Saturday should accommodate 12-15 people.

Details

Please send price information for 12 double rooms, meals and meeting room with overhead, screen and flip chart to my attention at the above address. I would also appreciate any information you have on tourist attractions in Chicago.

Request

Sincerely,

Signature

Thomas A. Wood
President

TAW:cl

10

Confirmation to Speaker

This letter confirms speaking arrangements that have been discussed earlier.

Clerks Unlimited
P.O. Box 245 • Eugene, OR 97405

May 9, 20XX

Thomas A. Smith
P.O. Box 1234
Valparaiso, IN 46383

Dear Mr. Smith:

Thank you for agreeing to speak at our Professional Proofreaders' April meeting. As we discussed Tuesday morning, the group meets the third Thursday of each month at 6:30 p.m. at the Westport Grill. I hope you will be able to join the group for dinner before you speak at 7:30 p.m.

Details (specific)

We are looking forward to you sharing some of the tips and techniques you use as well as answering some grammar questions for us.

Information (general)

There will be an overhead projector and screen as you requested. Please plan on speaking about 30 minutes, and then allow 15 to 20 minutes more to answer questions from the group.

Details (specific)

Mr. Smith, if you have any questions or need more information, please contact me at 555-3498.

Contact Information

Sincerely,

Signature

Ida Johns
Program Coordinator

Giving Information

This memo informs employees of a change in the company medical insurance plan and gives information and a contact for information.

MEMORANDUM

Date: September 18, 20XX
To: All Employees
From: Martha Landers, Office Manager
Re: Change in Health Insurance Provider

Beginning October 1, First Coverage will be the health insurance provider for our employees.

Information

Although few changes will occur as a result of our switching health insurance coverage, you should note that First Coverage designates certain medical professionals as "preferred providers." These individuals have agreed to accept predetermined fees for certain services. While our employees are free to choose their health-care provider, fees will generally be lower when using preferred providers. This will result in lower costs to you on services not covered in our policy or performed before individual deductions are met.

Details

Detailed insurance information will be distributed to all employees when our new policy becomes effective October l. In the meantime, if you have any questions regarding this change, please contact me at ext. 432.

Contact Information

10

Discontinuing Business Relationships

This letter expresses appreciation for good work, but at the same time informs the reader that the job is ending.

10

Valley View Shops
P.O. Box 5310
Aurora, CO 80013

June 1, 20XX

Sharon Young
Right On! Writing
P.O. Box 6864
Boulder, CO 80322

Dear Sharon:

Enclosed is a summary of the team-building workshop evaluations. We are very pleased with the results and feel you met our expectations extremely well. Thank you for tailoring the course with our materials in order to meet our objectives.

Thank You

Even with all the good feedback, however, the money we need in order to schedule additional workshops with you is not available. Hopefully next year will be another story, and the two of us can plan more skill-development workshops for the secretaries.

Negative News

Future Option

Again, it was a pleasure working with you. I am enclosing a "to whom it may concern" reference that states how highly we regard your work.

Goodwill

Sincerely,

Signature

Bernice Kendrick
Supervisor, Purchasing Services

Enc.

This is a follow-up letter to a client who has canceled work. This letter helps maintain the relationship and sets the stage for more work in the future.

Managing Your Time — for Yourself! Workshops

Plaza Parkway Building
P.O. Box 5130
Salem, OR 97304

May 31, 20XX

Joyce Roland
Training and Development
Perry Stores
P.O. Box 312
Salem, OR 97304

Dear Joyce:

Thank you for letting me know this far in advance that you will not be scheduling additional workshops in "Managing Your Time — for Yourself!"

Thank You
Goodwill

I have enjoyed my work with the groups from Perry Stores and feel the workshops were productive for your staff. Perhaps there will be an opportunity in the future to plan a workshop with you on another aspect of skill development: telephone techniques, getting organized or presentational speaking. I'll call you next quarter.

General Comments

Specific Follow-Up

In the meantime, all the best to you and Susan. Thank you again!

Personal Note
Thank You

Sincerely,

Signature

Barbara Dennis

Rejecting a Request

This letter turns down a request, but it begins and ends on a positive note.

General Corporation
253 West 12th Street
Somerset, NJ 08873

February 25, 20XX

Robert P. Thomas
General Corporation District IV
P.O. Box 6425
Raleigh, NC 27628

Robert:

Thank you for the good work you did in preparing your district's 20XX budget. You supplied all the information I needed to make decisions regarding which equipment will be replaced this year.

Thank You

I agree with you that three-fourths of all your road equipment should be replaced. However, we are not able to do it this year; the best I can promise is a new mixer and spreader.

Agreement
Negative News

Hopefully next year the company will be able to replace more of your equipment. The budget dollars should be similar. Let me know if I can do anything to help keep your equipment operating efficiently for one more year.

Option
Goodwill

Harry King

Introducing a New Employee

This introduces a new staff member to the department.

MEMORANDUM

TO: Department Staff
FROM: Janice

Please welcome Susan James to ABC's marketing
department. Susan will begin working with us on April 14 as
staff assistant to Bill Baker — replacing Marge Williams.

Susan has been with ABC for three years, greeting everyone
from behind the front reception desk. Please help Susan by
answering any questions she may have about the work in our
department.

Janice T.

Purpose
Details

Request

10

Checklist

- Did you use a positive tone?
- Does the letter specify the terms of employment?
- Does the letter request specific information?
- Did you summarize, thank or restate in the last part of the letter?
- If you received the letter, would you know what to do?
- Does your letter show respect for confidentiality?
- Is your letter personal and courteous?

10

CHAPTER 11

Customer Relations Letters

Letters that improve or maintain good customer relations sell a company's image. The broad categories are as follows:

- General Appreciation
- Acknowledging a Complaint
- Following Up on a Complaint
- Regaining a Customer's Confidence
- Acknowledging a Complaint — Disclaiming Responsibility
- Acknowledging a Complaint — Explaining a Misunderstanding
- Correcting an Error
- General Apology
- Acknowledging an Order — Back Order
- Acknowledging an Order — Explaining Shipment Procedures
- Apologizing for an Employee's Action
- Notifying Customers of a Move
- Holiday Greetings
- Notification of Complaints

11

At the side of the page, you will find a brief explanation of each part of the letter. The first letter identifies each section of the letter. Subsequent letters identify only changes to the basic format.

Step-by-Step Guide

These letters are designed to improve or maintain customer relations. The maxim that the customer is always right should be kept in mind while writing these letters. At times, however, you may have to let the customer think he is right while you are proving him wrong!

Step 1: The first part of the letter states your purpose. This may be anything from acknowledging a complaint to notifying a customer of a move.

Step 2: The second part of the letter explains the purpose. If the first part acknowledges a complaint, then the second part explains what you are going to do about it. If the first part announces a new address to valued customers, then the second part gives the details about the new location's conveniences.

Step 3: The last part is the sugar to leave a good taste in the customer's mouth. It summarizes the letter, thanks the customer and reiterates the customer's value to your organization.

Note: At the end of this chapter is a checklist to use when you write a customer relations letter.

General Appreciation

This letter is used to show appreciation for your customers. It may be used as a sales and promotional letter or a thank you for continued patronage.

Zebra Prints 224 Bever Ave. • Madrid, MS 39378	*Letterhead*
January 12, 20XX	*Date*
Lillian R. Wilkinson 4500 Ramble Road Lane Madrid, MS 39379	*Inside Address*
Dear Ms. Wilkinson:	*Salutation*
On behalf of Zebra Prints, we wish to express our sincerest appreciation for your continued patronage. It is because of valued customers like you that we are able to continue to offer you the finest in fabrics.	*Statement of Purpose* *Compliment*
Zebra Prints has been in business for 75 years. We are dedicated to bringing you the finest in fabrics, particularly those of all-natural materials. Mr. Case, our founding father, loved to say, "The customer wants the best at the lowest price," and that is the motto we use as our guiding principle.	*Elaboration*
Please stop in and see us soon. Our new spring fabrics will be in the showroom on March 15. If you bring this letter with you, we will give you a 15 percent discount on any fabric you purchase in March.	*Summary* *Benefit*
Sincerely yours,	*Complimentary Close*
Signature	*Signature*
Terrance Sullivan Case, Jr. President	*Typed Name*
TSC:maj	*Additional Information*

11

Acknowledging a Complaint

This letter is used to acknowledge a complaint and offer a solution to the problem.

11

Tiny Toes Dance Studio
33 Barbara Dr. • Butte, MT 59777

September 2, 20XX

Mickey Wu
790 7th St.
Butte, MT 59777

Dear Mr. Wu:

Thank you for your letter of August 30 discussing our policy concerning payment for missed classes.

Acknowledgment of Complaint

I have checked with our owner, Ms. Timberlane, for a clarification. In the past, our policy was that missed classes would still need to be paid for. Under the circumstances, however, she said that you will not have to pay for the classes your daughter missed because of her unfortunate accident on the way to class.

Solution

We hope this is a satisfactory solution for you and wish your daughter, Jasmine, a speedy recovery. We shall put a hold on your account until she is ready to return to her tap lessons. Thank you once again for your concern.

Summary

Thank You

Sincerely yours,

Signature

Mary Manson
Business Manager

MLM:wmj

Following Up on a Complaint

Once a complaint is logged and your company has resolved it, send a follow-up letter as an extra effort toward redeeming your reputation for good service. Here is an example.

McGiven Publishing Company
29 New York Ave.
New York, NY 10022

May 21, 20XX

Steve Laing
444 Madison St.
Livingston, NJ 07039

Dear Mr. Laing:

Our service goal is to fill your orders accurately 100 percent of the time. However, when we fall short and errors occur, it's frustrating for everyone.

Goal
Acknowledgment of Error

I'm sorry you had a problem with your recent order, and I hope the situation has been resolved to your satisfaction. If there is anything else we can do for you, please call us toll-free at 800-555-5225 Monday through Friday between 7 a.m. and 4 p.m. Eastern time.

Apology
Goodwill
Assistance Offer
Contact Information

Thanks for your patience and understanding.

Thanks

Sincerely,

Signature

Peg Mahr
Customer Service Manager

PM:hs

11

Regaining a Customer's Confidence

The key to regaining a customer's confidence is to respond promptly to a customer's complaint, whether the problem has been corrected yet or not. Always maintain professionalism when referring to the responsibility for the problem — never assign individual blame. Instead, report a positive action being taken to avoid future problems.

Begin by acknowledging the problem specifically. Report what will be or is being done to correct the problem. Then, assure the customer or client that his business is appreciated and you are still interested in continuing the relationship.

11

Modern Medical Supplies
302 Main • Portland, OR 97272

November 23, 20XX

Dr. Laura Schmitt
1520 Barston Blvd.
Sacramento, CA 95808

Dear Dr. Schmitt:

Please accept our sincerest apologies for the recent mix-up with the shipment of tongue depressors. I can assure you that action has been taken to remedy the problem in our warehouse.	*Statement of Purpose*
As a token of good faith, we have deducted 15 percent from your bill. We hope this will help compensate for any inconvenience this problem caused. Because of this unfortunate situation, we have discovered a number of errors with our shipping department. Consequently, we have	*Regaining of Confidence*
brought in a new person to head this department. We are confident that our new shipping clerk will keep things running smoothly for you and	*Result*
all of our customers. Thank you for bringing the error to our attention.	*Thank You*
We hope this will be a satisfactory solution. Your corrected order of tongue depressors should be arriving shortly, as they were sent November 22.	*Summary of Order Information*

Sincerely yours,

Signature

Graham Johnson
Customer Relations

GJJ:amr

Acknowledging a Complaint — Disclaiming Responsibility

This letter acknowledges a customer's complaint in order to maintain good relations; however, it refers the customer to another source that is responsible for the problem.

Peoria Pet Foods
3005 Lincolnway • Peoria, IL 61635

March 30, 20XX

Mary Louise Jones
Paws R Us
8900 Waconia
Joliet, IL 60434

Dear Ms. Jones:

Thank you for bringing the problem of late deliveries to our attention. I'm sure they must be most aggravating. — *Acknowledgment of Complaint*

As much as we would like to help you, the problem lies with the trucking firm. We have contacted them concerning the late deliveries and are reviewing our use of Nelson Trucking as our carrier. At present, we have no contract with them but shall be demanding a contract so that we have leverage in such matters. I suggest that you contact them, also, to emphasize the seriousness of the situation. — *Disclaimer of Responsibility* / *Action Taken* / *Result* / *Suggestion*

I'm sorry I can't help you any more than this, but I can assure you that we are trying to remedy the situation as quickly as we can. Unfortunately, an immediate solution is dependent upon Nelson Trucking. Thank you once again for your understanding. — *Apology* / *Thank You*

Sincerely yours,

Signature

Lucy McAlister
Customer Relations

LJM:glu

11

Acknowledging a Complaint — Explaining a Misunderstanding

Acknowledge a customer's complaint in order to maintain good relations by explaining a misunderstanding between the customer and the business.

11

RTM, Inc.
P.O. Box 2089 • Milwaukee, WI 53219

January 16, 20XX

Thomas R. Linder
Bottlers' Distributors
7035 Wacker
Milwaukee, WI 53227

Dear Mr. Linder:

I appreciate you bringing to my attention the problem of our Colden Beer and its introductory flyer. I understand your confusion perfectly.

Acknowledgment of Complaint

When we sent you the letter introducing our new beer, our marketing department mistakenly sent a mock-up of an ad for Eagle's Wings Ale. Naturally, you would be confused because we were referring to the blue eagle on Colden Beer while giving you the bald eagle label of Eagle's Wings Ale. We are most sorry for this error and have enclosed a corrected flyer.

Explain Misunderstanding

Apology

I hope this letter and the enclosed corrected flyer clear up this unfortunate misunderstanding. Thank you once again for bringing this to my attention.

Thank You

Sincerely,

Signature

R. Edwards Rands
Public Relations Director

RER:kks

Correcting an Error

Correct an error that either the customer or the business caught.

Capital Credit Union
890 Minnesota Ave. • Washington, D.C. 20041

April 24, 20XX

Mr. and Mrs. John Gallup
3256 Mozart Dr.
Silver Spring, MD 20743

Dear Mr. and Mrs. Gallup:

After our recent auditing, we discovered an underpayment to your account of $53.23 in interest. | *Statement of Error*

The error occurred in the transferring of funds in March from your High-Fi account to your regular savings account. We have corrected your savings account and credited you with $53.23. | *Explanation* / *Correction*

I hope this is satisfactory, and I apologize for any confusion this error caused. Thank you for your continued patronage. | *Apology* / *Thank You*

Sincerely,

Signature

Molly Butters
Vice President, Accounting

MMB:tli

11

General Apology

This letter is used to apologize to customers.

Merker's Department Store
1115 Brandon • New Ulm, MN 56053

July 22, 20XX

Kim Langworth
R.R. 1
Red Earth, MN 56670

Dear Ms. Langworth:

We at Merker's would like to extend our sincerest apologies
and ask for your understanding.

Apology

Our recent sales brochure made claims that we could not
follow through on. Not all merchandise in the Summer Saver
Sale was on sale at 50 percent off. The printer inadvertently
left out the important word "selected." Because of this
glaring error, we have decided to postpone our sale and
reschedule it for another time. By postponing the sale, we
will be able to offer you even better bargains than we had
originally planned.

Explanation

Decision

Benefit

Thank you for your understanding in this embarrassing
situation.

Thank You

Sincerely,

Signature

R. Merker
Chairman of the Board

RCM:hhh

11

Acknowledging an Order — Back Order

This letter is used to acknowledge that a customer's order has been received but that it is back-ordered, thus causing a delay.

Todmann Nuts and Bolts
P.O. Box 3445 • Idaho Falls, ID 83406

June 3, 20XX

Timothy R. Johnson, Purchasing
Sheppard Hardware Distributors
P.O. Box 1078
Kansas City, MO 64109-1078

Dear Mr. Johnson:

We were pleased to receive your order for 10,000 quarter-inch nuts, part number XK22345JM. However, we are unable at this time to fulfill the order. — *Acknowledgment of Order*

Our present inventory has been depleted, and that nut is now on back order until mid-July. Our supplier of raw materials is unable to supply the materials until July 1, thus pushing us back to mid-July for possible delivery. We have tried without success to find an alternate source of raw materials. — *Explanation*

If you like, we could substitute part number XK22346JM. It is a penny higher in price per unit. Otherwise, we will keep your order and rush it to you as soon as we can start production on these nuts again. Please let us know your preference this week. — *Alternative (optional)*

Thank you for your understanding in this matter. We apologize for your inconvenience. — *Thank You Apology*

Sincerely,

Signature

Cass Walker
Production Head

CBW:pst

11

Acknowledging an Order — Explaining Shipment Procedures

Explain a shipping procedure to a customer while acknowledging that an order has been received.

11

Raging Bull Farms
R.R. 2 • Kingman, OK 73439

August 13, 20XX

Natalie Gorman
Cherokee Crafts
900 E. Main
Tulsa, OK 74102

Dear Ms. Gorman:

Thank you for your order of 25 authentic Cherokee head-dresses on August 11, 20XX. We will be sending those immediately. | *Acknowledgment of Order*

Because of the fragile nature of our headdresses, we hand deliver to our customers within Oklahoma. Our delivery day for Tulsa is Friday, which means that your headdresses will arrive this coming Friday, August 17. If this is unsatisfactory, please call us so that we can arrange an alternative delivery date. | *Explanation*

Action Plan

Alternative Plan

Thank you for your business. I'm sure you will be most pleased with our headdresses, and we look forward to working with you in the future. | *Thank You*

Sincerely yours,

Signature

Tamara Whitewater

TJW:zmd

Apologizing for an Employee's Action

Apologize for the action of one of your employees who has damaged customer relations.

Refrain from naming the employee and, if possible, explain the alternative plan you have chosen for the employee. Unless there are chronic problems, it is in the company's best interest to illustrate compassion for its clients and employees.

Belle's Phone Store
Windale Mall
8855 Outer Dr. • Waukegan, IL 60079

November 3, 20XX

Travis C. Schultz
5554 Rocky Shore Dr.
North Waukegan, IL 60079

Dear Mr. Schultz:

I wish to personally apologize for your unfortunate treatment by one of our employees last Friday. His actions toward you were totally inappropriate. | *Apology*

Because of this situation, the employee has been placed in a position working directly with our inventory, having less contact with customers. We would also like to offer you a $50 gift certificate for merchandise at our store. We value our customers and hope this token will help compensate for the embarrassment you felt. We are increasing our training in customer relations for all of our employees to avoid just such a problem occurring again. | *Action Taken (optional)* / *Goal of Customer Satisfaction* / *Result*

Thank you for your business and your understanding. We hope this is a satisfactory solution to the problem. | *Thank You*

Sincerely yours,

Signature

Belle June Maples

BJM:kio

Notifying Customers of a Move

Notify customers of a move and assure them that the move either will not affect them or will be advantageous to them.

11

Marco Paper Clips
P.O. Box 22 • Marquette, MI 49855

May 4, 20XX

K.J. Wasserman
City Business Supply
763 C. St. S.W.
Columbia, MO 65205

Dear Mr. Wasserman:

On July 1, 20XX, Marco Paper Clips will be moving to Des Moines, Iowa. This move should greatly benefit your company.

Announcement

We are excited about the move to Des Moines. Our move will help you receive shipments more quickly. It will also reduce the cost of shipping to Marco, and we can pass those savings on to you. Des Moines' larger labor market also allows us to expand our facilities and product line. We feel this will definitely benefit our customers.

Elaboration

Benefits

Please feel free to contact us if you have any concerns. Our new address in Des Moines will be: Marco Paper Clips, 3567 Grandview, Des Moines, IA 54421. Our toll-free number will be 800-BUY-CLIP.

Summary

Contact Information

Sincerely,

Signature

G. Antonio Marco
President

GAM:etv

Holiday Greetings

This letter is used to send holiday greetings to your customers. It is preferable to use personal stationery or a notecard especially designed for the situation.

Flatt Tire Co.
223 Nueva Matica • Santa Cruz, CA 95066

December 5, 20XX

Dear Mr. Brown:

Flatt Tire Co. would like to wish you and your employees the very best this holiday season. We hope that your establishment has been blessed with exceptional customers, as we have.

Greetings

We are most fortunate to have customers like Glendale Amoco and hope that, during this coming new year, we can continue our relationship. We know our prosperity depends on our customers.

Elaboration (optional)

Thank you for helping make Flatt Tire Co. one of the leaders in Southern California. Our fondest regards for all of you at Glendale Amoco.

Thank You Goodwill

Happy Holidays,

Signature

Rhonda J. Flatt
President

11

Notification of Complaints

This letter asks for a solution to a complaint of faulty merchandise but ends on a business-as-usual note to maintain the professional contact.

PAM'S PARTY GIFTS
P.O. Box 8473
Torrance, CA 90502

April 18, 20XX

Delta Novelty Company
3217 SW 31st St.
Topeka, KS 66614

SUBJECT: REQUEST FOR CREDIT IN ACCOUNT

The case of Hippity Holiday Bunnies that I purchased from your company do not hop. I am, therefore, returning them to you and requesting that you credit my account for the amount charged plus shipping.

Reason
Request
(specific)

The Hippity Holiday Bunnies that arrived at my store had faulty mechanisms which caused them to fall over instead of hop — as promised in your sales brochure. Because I plan on selling off my line of seasonal items within the next three weeks, I wish my account to be issued a credit instead of you replacing the faulty merchandise. Please find enclosed the copies of your invoice, #1342, in the amount of $36 and my invoice for shipping charges of $2.95.

Details

Enclosure

Your quality products have always sold well in my store, and I look forward to seeing your new line of fall items as soon as they are available. In the meantime, your prompt attention to this matter is appreciated.

Agreement

Request
(general)

Martha Sacks

Enc.

11

In this letter, the writer assumes part of the responsibility, but states clearly what is expected in the future.

7136 Dartmouth Ave. (2E)
St. Louis, MO 63130-3008

May 28, 20XX

Brad Smith
Ralph's Restaurant
22nd & Market
St. Louis, MO 63103

Dear Mr. Smith:

I am writing because of my disappointment with the choice of dessert served to the League of Successful Professionals at our dinner meeting May 23. I do not believe that popsicles are an appropriate dessert at a business gathering such as ours.

Purpose

The quality of the food and service at our meetings is generally very good. This is the reason we continue to use your facilities, and why I was surprised by the dessert. I may not have been specific enough when we reviewed the menu. Though we discussed in detail the items to be included on the dinner buffet, dessert was simply defined in our contract as "a frozen ice cream item to be served individually." I should have been more detailed in my request.

Agreement

Responsibility (shared)

Please see that I am given a specific menu for our July meeting by June 25 so that I may review it before signing the service contract. This will help avoid any future misunderstandings.

Request

Sincerely,

Signature

Katherine Taylor

11

This letter requests a solution to the complaint. The letter backs up the request with documentation of the problem and a specific date for it to be resolved.

A-1 Merchandise Supply Company
P.O. Box 1276
Grandview, MO 64030

May 11, 20XX

Taylor Jackson
Jackson Roofing Contractors
P.O. Box 5692
Grandview, MO 64031

RE: Roof repair, invoice #1724, March 11, 20XX

Dear Mr. Jackson:

The roof, which you repaired in March, continues to leak along the south wall of our overstock merchandise storage area. Please repair the roof by June 1, 20XX, without charge, as stated in your two-year guarantee.

Reason
Request

Bill Wagstone, a repairman with your company, has examined the roof and informed me that the new seals placed between the roof and the surrounding brick walls were not properly installed. Mr. Wagstone has advised me that the roof will continue to leak until this problem is corrected.

Details

Fortunately, before the last storm, we were able to move the merchandise out of the area before any damage was done. My company cannot afford the loss of this storage space, however, so all additional repairs must be completed by June l.

Details

Please contact me the week of May 25 so that I will know when to expect your roofers.

Request

Sincerely,

Signature

Anne Smith
President

This letter asks a shopkeeper to act on the request of neighbors.

The Itty Bitty Shoppe
1934 Longan • Bartlesville, OK 74006

February 15, 20XX

Patricia Wolfe
1936 Longan
Bartlesville, OK 74006

Dear Ms. Wolfe:

The cold weather season approaches, and I would like to inform you that all shopkeepers are expected to keep the walk in front of their stores free of snow. Five other merchants, myself included, have had a problem with your lack of responsibility in this matter. It inconveniences customers and merchants alike. | *Introduction*

Please help us keep the walk free of snow during the winter months by clearing off the area in front of your store. | *Request*

Until now, we have taken care of our own space — and when a neighbor needed help, we all pitched in. This year we are reminding you — before the shovels are all sold and the salt is all used — that everyone is expected to keep the sidewalk in front of his or her store free of snow and ice. This is not only for ease of walking, but also for safety. | *Background* *Reason*

Thanks from your neighbors and the customers who come by on snow days! | *Goodwill*

Signature

Janice Smith/The Itty Bitty Shoppe

11

This letter notifies a business of a complaint.

JRD, Inc.
P.O. Box 6864
Mission, Kansas 66202

December 12, 20XX

Mr. Anton Drissler, General Manager
Scripps
4732 Pennslyvania
Kansas City, MO 64112

Dear Mr. Drissler:

I am writing about the facilities, food and service at the holiday dinner that JRD Corporation gave for its employees on Tuesday evening, December 11, at Scripps.

Reason

First, Ballroom B was much too cold for comfortable dining, with several very strong drafts along the west wall. Audio systems at parties in Ballrooms A and C were loud and distracting for our entertainers as well as our guests.

Negatives

Second, the food service was extremely poor — we had contracted for dinner at 6:30 p.m., and the first guests were not served until 8 p.m. The main course was cold; our ice cream dessert was melted.

Specific Details

Third, there was no one available from Sales and Catering to offer help, and those we talked to at the front desk were "not responsible."

In order to repair the situation, please reduce our room rent and food bill by one-half; I have enclosed our agreement with the original total. And please, always have a representative from Sales and Catering in attendance at any future function hosted by JRD at Scripps.

Solution

For over 10 years, JRD has hosted many occasions in your hotel. In light of our long professional association, I appreciate your resolution of this matter.

Appreciation of Resolution

Sincerely,

Signature

Janet Coen
for Thomas W. Smith, President

11

This letter gives notification of a claim for damages made during an office move.

TIMBER Manufacturing
P.O. Box 5557
Atlanta, GA 30329

April 29, 20XX

Mr. Richard Lyons, President
Great Movers
P.O. Box 5748
Atlanta, GA 30327

Dear Mr. Lyons:

This is to notify you of our claim for damaged goods against Great Movers. On April 27, Timber Manufacturing moved its office from 12224 Grand to 22455 McGee. The order number with Great Movers was #89648.

Purpose
Details

As the furniture was unloaded and placed in the new office, I discovered a 12-inch scratch along the front of an enameled cabinet (picture enclosed). I plan on having the damage to this expensive piece repaired immediately and have enclosed five cost estimates for the work. All are rather close in price, but I prefer using Addison's as they have done repairs for me in the past and guarantee their work. Addison's estimate to repair the enameled cabinet is $750.

Reasons

Decision

My contract with you covers loss or damage to $1,000. Please send your check for repairing the damage ($750) to:

Solution

> Donald J. Bilyeu
> President
> Timber Manufacturing
> P.O. Box 5557
> Atlanta, GA 30329

Sincerely,

Signature

Donald J. Bilyeu

DJB:efk
Enc.

11

Checklist

- Did you use a positive tone?
- Does the letter make the customer feel like he is valuable?
- Did you introduce the topic of the letter in the first part?
- Did you include all of the necessary details for the customer?
- Did you include a telephone number, if appropriate, so the client can reach you?
- Did you offer a solution to the problem?
- Did you take the initiative in the letter for the action you desire?
- Did you include all background information or details necessary in the second part of the letter so the client understands the letter?
- Did you summarize, thank or apologize again in the last part of the letter?
- If you received the letter, how would you feel?

11

Media Letters

Here are samples to help you write letters to the media (newspapers, television stations, magazines). The broad categories are as follows:

- Media Event Letter — Sales Campaign Kickoff
- Media Event Letter — Recently Published Book
- Media Event Letter — Anniversary
- Press Release — Anniversary
- Press Release — Speaking Engagement
- Press Release — Promotion
- Press Release — New Employee
- Response to Editorial — Positive
- Response to Editorial — Negative
- Letter Asking to Make a Speech
- Letter Asking for a Correction

At the side of the page, you will find a brief explanation of each part of the letter. The first letter identifies each section of the letter. Subsequent letters identify only changes to the basic format.

Step-by-Step Guide

Media letters are used in business as a way to get the public's attention. Media exposure is free advertising, and the smart businessperson uses it to sell her business and its services or products. The letter in and of itself is a sales tool.

Step 1: The first part of the letter or press release states your purpose. This may be anything from announcing a new employee to responding to an editorial.

Step 2: The second part of the letter or press release explains the first part by giving details and examples about the first part. This part should include all pertinent information concerning the event or situation. If, for example, you are announcing a new employee, you would give the details about the employee in the second part. Always answer who, what, when, where, why and, if appropriate, how, in this section.

Step 3: The last part of the letter acts as a summary, reminding the recipient of the general nature of the letter. It may also be used as a thank you.

Note: At the end of this chapter is a checklist to use when you write a media letter.

Media Event Letter — Sales Campaign Kickoff

Alert the media to a sales campaign kickoff and invite the media to cover the event.

Capital Crystal 449 Worthington • Charleston, WV 25009	*Letterhead*
March 2, 20XX	*Date*
Todd Phillips, Station Manager KOAL 2525 Kanawah Charleston, WV 25009	*Inside Address*
Dear Mr. Phillips:	*Salutation*
On March 25, Capital Crystal will announce the winner of our "How Many Goblets in a Dump Truck" contest. We will do so at noon in front of our business at 449 Worthington.	*Announcement*
Our "How Many Goblets in a Dump Truck" contest has been going on now for approximately three months, and one of the more than 4,000 entrants will be the lucky winner of $1,000. We will also donate $1,000 to Charleston's Homeless Shelter at that time. During the announcement, we will dump the goblets out of the truck and onto the ground. Wade Wilson and His Debonaires will play during the reception that follows.	*Explanation* *Specific Details*
We are sure that this event will be of interest to your viewers of "Eye on Charleston" at noon because of the huge response we have had to the contest. Thank you for your interest.	*Summary* *Thank You*
Sincerely yours,	*Complimentary Close*
Signature	*Signature*
Candice Trotter President	*Typed Name*
CJT:lsj	*Additional Information*

12

215

Media Event Letter — Recently Published Book

Notify the media of a recently published book.

Donaldson's
223 Niagara Dr. • Buffalo, NY 14290

September 12, 20XX

Mary Beth Parkinson
WWJ
874 7th St.
Buffalo, NY 14292

Dear Ms. Parkinson:

I recently published a book called *Entrepreneur at Risk*. I am sending you a copy to review.

Announcement

The topic is worthy of your morning show, "Good Morning Buffalo," and I would be interested in discussing the book as a guest on your show. The premise is that entrepreneurs are at risk in the U.S. and will soon be an endangered species. This is a very timely topic, as there is an upcoming forum on entrepreneurs at the Carmine Colosseum.

Explanation

Persuasion

I have enclosed my biographical sketch, a synopsis of the book and a press release from my publishing house. I hope that you will take the time to look at these. Thank you for your attention.

Summary

Thank You

Sincerely,

Signature

Larry J. Beiers
President

LJB:wuy

Media Event Letter — Anniversary

Use this letter to alert the media of your company's anniversary.

Evanson Buick
7793 Sahara Way • Reno, NV 89585

May 19, 20XX

Wayne Wilson
KBET
444 Plaza Dr.
Reno, NV 89588

Dear Mr. Wilson:

Evanson Buick will be turning 50 years old on May 29, making us the oldest car dealership in Nevada. We will be staging a three-day celebration.

Announcement

On May 29, we will kick off our anniversary with free hot-air balloon rides and an ascension at 6 p.m. On May 30, we will have the oldest race car driver, Judd MacElroy, signing autographs from 2 to 4 p.m. On May 31, we will have our drawing for a Buick Reatta at 5:30 p.m., followed by a picnic open to the public. During all three days, there will be displays of antique autos and carnival rides for the children. We think that our anniversary event would make a fine spot on your "Neighbors" segment on the 6 o'clock news.

Explanation

Specific Details

I have enclosed a flyer describing the complete festivities. Thank you for helping us celebrate our anniversary.

Summary
Thank You

Sincerely,

Signature

M. Art Evanson
President

MAE:fsw
Enc.

12

217

Press Release — Anniversary

Use this press release to alert the media of a company's anniversary.

Darling's Cookies
309 Watertown Road • Tacoma, WA 98438

January 19, 20XX
FOR IMMEDIATE RELEASE

On February 5, 20XX, Darling's Cookies will celebrate its 50th anniversary, making us the oldest bakery in Tacoma.

Darling's Cookies was established on February 5, 195X, by Darrel Darling. At first, Darling's employed only three people and was located on Front Street in downtown Tacoma. After the war, Darling's moved to its present location on Watertown Road and now employs 25 people full-time. Darling's specialties are cinnamon rolls, chocolate chip cookies and its patented double chocolate fudge bar. Darling's will host an open house on February 5 at its plant. We are expecting children from several local schools, residents from several nursing homes and group houses, as well as our regular patrons. Please stop by for free refreshments.

FOR MORE INFORMATION, CONTACT:
Darrel Darling, Jr.
President
555-2211

Announcement

Explanation

Specific Details

Contact Information

12

Press Release — Speaking Engagement

Use this press release to alert the media of an upcoming speech.

Los Gatos Community College
2312 College Dr. • Los Gatos, NM 87531
505-555-6636

April 2, 20XX
FOR IMMEDIATE RELEASE

Dr. Larry Thompson, noted historian, will speak April 20, 20XX, at Los Gatos Community College. He will speak on "History in the Making: How Current Events Redefine Our Lives."

Dr. Thompson is a leading authority on trends in history. He is professor of history from Cornell University in Ithaca, New York. He is presently on leave from the university so he can lecture around the world on this topic. His speech has been well-received throughout the United States. He will explain how the fall of the Berlin Wall has affected all of us. After the speech, Dr. Thompson will hold a symposium on American business trends. He will autograph copies of his best seller, *Wake Up, America*, in the lobby of the Emerson Auditorium prior to his speech at 7 p.m.

FOR MORE INFORMATION, CONTACT:
Sara Thompson
Public Relations Department
Los Gatos Community College

Announcement

Topic

Explanation

Specific Details

Contact Information

12

Press Release — Promotion

Use this press release to notify the media of a promotion within your business.

Ogden Manufacturing
58 Brigham Young Dr. • Ogden, UT 84404
801-555-9889

August 30, 20XX
FOR IMMEDIATE RELEASE

Ogden Manufacturing announces the promotion of Paul K. Van Daan to Vice President, Accounting. He will replace Terrance Reilly, who is retiring.

Announcement

Paul Van Daan joined Ogden Manufacturing in March 19XX as an accountant and was promoted in 19XX to Department Head, Accounts Receivable. In 20XX, he was promoted to Division Head, Customer Relations. He is a graduate of Brigham Young University and is a Certified Public Accountant. Previously, he worked for Dowling Box, Ltd.

Explanation

Specific Details

FOR MORE INFORMATION, CONTACT:
Dana Conrad
Human Resources Office
Ogden Manufacturing

Contact Information

A black-and-white photo is enclosed.

Press Release — New Employee

Use this press release to announce to the media that a new employee will be joining your firm.

KLINGER BLINDS
2221 Washington • Flagstaff, AZ 86093

October 17, 20XX
FOR IMMEDIATE RELEASE

Klinger Blinds announces that Karen M. Bark has been hired as our director of sales. She will start in her new position on November 1.

Announcement

Karen M. Bark is a native of Southern California and was previously employed by Tremore Window Treatments in Los Angeles as sales coordinator. She has a degree in interior design from the Design Institute in San Francisco. Ms. Bark's design for *Home Lovely's* "Home Beautification Project" won first place last year in the prestigious competition.

Explanation

Specific Details

FOR MORE INFORMATION, CONTACT:
Trish Klinger
Klinger Blinds

Contact Information

A black-and-white photo is enclosed.

12

Response to Editorial — Positive

Use this letter to respond to an editorial when your firm agrees.

12

Greater Augusta Merchants
651 Main • Augusta, ME 04326

September 22, 20XX

Bonnie Ervin, Station Director
WKLT Radio
1500 Walker
Augusta, ME 04325

Dear Ms. Ervin:

We, the Greater Augusta Merchants, wish to commend you for the stand you have taken against parking meters in downtown Augusta. Your editorial of September 20 was well thought out.   *Announcement*

We feel that placing parking meters in downtown Augusta will discourage our customers from coming downtown to shop. Your report of other nearby cities who have recently installed parking meters and have seen a drop in customers demonstrates that parking meters could create the same problem if the city government passes this ordinance. We strongly urge you to continue to speak out against this issue.   *Explanation*

Specific Details

Thank you for your support of our position.   *Thank You*

Sincerely,

Signature

Marvin Quackenbush
Executive Secretary

MJQ:omr

Response to Editorial — Negative

Use this letter to respond to an editorial when your firm disagrees.

Greater Augusta Merchants
651 Main • Augusta, ME 04326

October 20, 20XX

Bonnie Ervin, Station Director
WKLT Radio
1500 Walker
Augusta, ME 04325

Dear Ms. Ervin:

Although we agree with your previous editorials opposing parking meters in downtown Augusta, we are not in agreement with your editorial of October 18. We can see no value in turning the downtown business district into a mall-like area.

Announcement

To resurface our streets and make them into malls will irreversibly damage businesses downtown. The city engineers estimate the mall project will disrupt business for a minimum of a full year. Many downtown businesses are now struggling to stay alive, and the mall project would be their death knell. Additionally, when completed, we would have 50 percent fewer parking places for our customers. Perhaps the downtown area does need cosmetic surgery, but not when it devastates the area's economy.

Explanation

Specific Details

Concession

Persuasion

Thank you for your understanding of our opposition. We hope that you will reconsider your position.

Thank You

Sincerely,

Signature

Marvin Quackenbush
Executive Secretary

MJQ:omr

12

223

Letter Asking to Make a Speech

Use this letter when you want to make a speech or presentation.

J.P. Gaslight and Co.
790 Eastern Ave. • Ithaca, NY 14743

May 7, 20XX

Calvin S. Snyder, Program Chairman
Environmental Institute
445 J. Ave., East
Lincoln, NE 68302

Dear Mr. Snyder:

I would like to be put on the program of the upcoming   *Request*
Environmental Institute Workshop in October 20XX, in
Chicago. My presentation on acid rain and its effect on the
northeastern United States fits in with your theme,
"Environmental Consequences."

I have enclosed an outline of my proposed presentation. As   *Explanation*
you can see, my recent research for our firm shows the
irreversible damage done to the northeastern United States
by acid rain. The presentation I have outlined was well-
received at the Global Earth Conference in Boston and last   *Specific Details*
week at the Toronto Conference for Environmental
Concerns. I have also enclosed a list of other presentations I   *Enclosures*
have given on environmental issues.

Thank you for your prompt consideration.   *Thank You*

Sincerely,

Signature

Tracy Whiteman
TKW:cap

Enc.

Letter Asking for a Correction

Use this letter to request that a correction be made from a published or broadcast report.

Williams and Sons
1002 Elm St. • Topeka, KS 66404

August 11, 20XX

Anne Church, Managing Editor
Topeka Times
333 Main
Topeka, KS 66402

Dear Ms. Church:

Your article about Williams and Sons in last Sunday's *Times* was most appreciated. However, there is one correction that needs to be made.

Correction

In the article you stated that Williams and Sons has grown 15 percent in the last year. In reality, we have grown 25 percent in the last year — 15 percent of that being in the last month. Perhaps this seems like a trivial matter, but the smaller number is negative publicity for Williams. Would you please make a correction in your upcoming business-news section this Sunday?

Explanation

Specific Details

Request

Thank you for your prompt consideration. We appreciate the fine job you have been doing.

Thank You
Goodwill

Sincerely,

Signature

C. Blake Williams
President

CBW:nbc

12

Checklist

- Did you use a positive tone?

- Does the letter sell itself?

- Did you introduce the topic of the letter in the first part?

- Did you include all of the necessary details for the media such as date, time and place of event?

- Did you include your name so you can be reached for verification?

- Did you include all background information or details necessary in the second part of the letter?

- Did you summarize or thank in the last part of the letter?

- If you received the letter, would you do what you are asking the recipient to do?

12

CHAPTER 13

Electronic Mail

Electronic mail, or e-mail, is a relatively new form of written communication in the business world. The use of e-mail meets the needs of the fast pace of business and society. There are advantages and disadvantages to its use. Speed and convenience are the primary advantages, while lack of privacy and security are its disadvantages. There are those in the business world who frown on the use of e-mail because of its informality. The number of errant e-mails and "junk mail" that have caused embarrassing situations for employees can attest to the opinions that it is an inappropriate form of correspondence. Therefore, use e-mail cautiously and courteously. This chapter will provide the tips and techniques for smart e-mail practices.

- Announcement of Meeting
- Message Verification
- Change in Client Status Announcement
- When to Use E-mail
- Request for Assistance
- Request for Materials Ordered
- Be Considerate
- Project Offer
- Follow-Up on Project

- Compliment to Employee for Work
- Etceteras: Smileys, Acronyms, Caps and "Flaming"
- Pros and Cons of E-mail Use

At the side of the page, you will find a brief explanation of each part of the e-mail. The first letter identifies each section of the message. Subsequent messages identify only changes to the basic format.

Step-by-Step Guide

Within a business, e-mail is primarily used to communicate internally, providing the user with the convenience of reaching many people quickly and simultaneously. It can be used to send notices to departments, update team members on a project or inform employees of benefits information or training opportunities. The e-mail letter can be printed by the recipient to be used for documentation. While humor and informality can be acceptable in this type of correspondence, the e-mail is strictly a tool for quick communication.

Step 1: Most e-mail servers have boxes that look similar to memo format. Complete the To and Subject boxes first. The server's software records the date and time the message was sent.

Step 2: Make a plan, then be brief and tell it like it is. A lot of e-mails that are sent off the cuff are followed by second and even third messages, trying to correct or update the information sent in the first. Take time to plan the message, and then be sure to carefully review it before hitting the send button!

This is one form of communication where the recipient expects you to get right to the point. Make your request or share your purpose in the first sentence.

Step 3: Keep it plain and simple. The message format that one person sends can often get scrambled in transmission, creating annoying effects for the recipient. Keep the format and the text simple to reduce the occurrence of garbled messages.

13

Step 4: Sign off. Because e-mails come with a From box, the recipient will know who has composed the message. You may or may not want to add a complimentary close and your name. Consider the recipient, the context of the message and whether this courtesy is applicable. Several options exist, including "Regards," "Thanks," or simply your initials.

Note: It's business!

Remember to be businesslike at all times. Write with clarity and effectiveness, use standard English and always be courteous!

Be careful when sending material that may be sensitive or confidential. Think of e-mail as a postcard — there is the potential for anyone to read it. Messages can be intercepted or forwarded, whether accidentally or intentionally, without your knowledge or consent.

At the end of this chapter is a checklist to use when you write an e-mail.

13

Announcement of Meeting

This e-mail is used by a supervisor to set up a series of meetings and to announce the first scheduled meeting.

To: Department Managers From: C. Jarrett Subject: Budget Meetings	*Send/Receive/Subject Information*
We will be meeting to plan the capital budgets for the coming year. I expect it will take three to four meetings for us to get the numbers on the table and then work them all out to the final projections.	*Announcement of Meeting*
The first meeting will be held on November 2 at 10 a.m. in the conference room. We will set the remaining meeting dates/times during this first one. Bring your department's budget projections and be prepared to explain how your department will contribute to the company's cost-cutting drive.	*Confirmation of Date, Time and Place* *Information Requested*
Thanks, Carl	*Complimentary Close and "Signature"*

13

Message Verification

Be sure to verify that your mail has been received, especially those messages deemed a high priority. E-mail networks, software and computers are not always reliable, and messages sometimes go undelivered. In addition, you are not likely to find out that the message was not delivered unless you take the time to verify through the "return receipt" box or another service that your e-mail software provides.

Change in Client Status Announcement

This message announces the change in status of a client and explains an unusual situation and how it is to be handled.

To: All Supervisory Personnel
From: D. Broadwik
Subject: TriState Industrial Services Account Status

Effective immediately: DO NOT SERVICE TriState Industrial Services.

TIS has dropped their contract with us, as of the end of last month. They are not entitled to any service. But evidently, word has not gotten around to all of TIS's personnel. We continue to get calls from their people.

Description of Status Change

Please make sure all staff members are aware of this change. This may be awkward, since many staff members have built relationships with people at TriState, but we cannot service a company that is no longer a client.

Additional Information

13

If anyone from TriState needs to discuss this, forward them to me at ext. 920 or to Seta Alvarez at 923.

Contact Information

Thanks for your help with this situation.

Duane Broadwik

When to Use E-mail

- To reach a lot of people quickly at the same time
- To send a short, personal message that doesn't require official letterhead and signature
- To send a message that does not need the security or confidentiality of traditional mail

Request for Assistance

This e-mail is used to direct all staff to help locate a missing file.

To: Human Resource Department Staff From: T. Mattieson Subject: Missing File on Capital Bank of Camden We are not able to locate the project file for Capital Bank of Camden. If you have borrowed it, have found it or have any idea where it may be, please call me ASAP at ext. 1310. Thanks! Terry	*Request*

Request for Materials Ordered

A direct e-mail can be a very effective way of making a quick, informal request.

To:	Roger Carlton	
From:	C. Celderon	
Subject:	Presentation Slides Not Delivered	

Roger,

You were going to have the presentation slides for the Cortland project to me by yesterday. They have not arrived.   *Request*

Please get in touch with me ASAP! We'll need those slides for tomorrow afternoon's presentation!

I left a voice mail with you this morning, too.   *Additional Information*

Charlie

13

Be Considerate

The more serious the message, the less appropriate the use of e-mail for communication. Bad news of any kind should never be sent via e-mail. Formal information can be altered, forged or duplicated easily in an e-mail format. Never send any communication that you would not be willing to say to someone's face. Always consider whether the joke or witty memo is one you would share with your boss before forwarding it on to someone else.

Project Offer

E-mail can be a quick way to informally offer a contract or project to an employee or outside client. As with any job offer, be sure to consider the e-mail message like a contract. Outline all of the essential information the person will need to make the decision to accept or reject the project.

To: Patrick Murphy
From: R. Jordan
Subject: Book Revision Project

Pat,

I have a book revision project if you're interested. The book is *Business Communication Made Easy*. It was last revised in 1993.

Offer Background

Revision points would include:
- Update form sections
- Update samples and language in samples
- Add section on e-mail
- Add any communication strategies for new or changed situations

Description of Project Goals

This would be work for hire. Turn around time is about two months (text in by Nov. 29). Fee is $3,600.

Fee and Time Frame

If you're interested, I'll overnight the book to you so that you can take a look at it. We need to have a contract on this by midweek.

Thanks,

Rich

Follow-Up on Project

E-mail is a convenient form of communication when sharing information is the primary purpose. A telephone call might take more time than is really necessary to simply share the information, and a formal letter would take more effort and resources than necessary.

The following is a message that describes the employee's plan of action and makes a request for input. The sender notes that an attachment will come with the message, making certain the receiver will look for it.

To: Rich Jordan
From: P. Murphy
Subject: Revision Outline

Rich:

I'm attaching the overall description of the plans I have for revision of the BCME project. I will begin working directly with the text that you sent me, but would like you to review these plans for your input/direction.

Notation of Attachment
State Purpose and Make Request

I will be adding additional information about the use of postcards to Chapter 3. And, I will work up a new chapter on informal business meetings (i.e., the coffeehouse, bookstore, etc.).

Additional Information About Plans

Unless something unforeseen should arise, I will expect this project to be wrapping up by the end of next week. Hope that will get it to your layout team with plenty of time to spare.

Time Frame

As always, your feedback is valuable and appreciated!

Murph

13

Compliment to Employee for Work

An e-mail can be a personal way to say thank you to someone for their great work on a project or proposal. The sender also has the option of forwarding copies of this acknowledgment to other members of the department as public recognition of the person's work.

To: R. Littleton
From: J. Griener
Subject: Thank you!

Ron:

Thank you for all the great work on the Masterson project! As you know, this was a really big one for our group, and it was thanks to you that the project got out the door on time.

I and everyone at MetroCom truly appreciate and applaud your work!

Best regards,

Jane

Acknowledgment of Work Well Done

Message of Appreciation

13

Etcetera ...

Smileys, or **emoticons**, are keyboard characters formed to create faces that express emotions. While some of the computer savvy find these expressions to be fun additions to e-mail correspondence, many consider them to be just too cute for business. Limit their use to recipients you're sure won't mind.

The use of **acronyms** and **online abbreviations** should be limited to familiar recipients, as well. Not everyone will be aware that IOW means "in other words," or that IMHO stands for "in my humble opinion."

Using **ALL CAPITAL LETTERS** is inappropriate for e-mail communication. Messages in all caps are much harder to read and indicate that you are shouting your message. Use capitals to STRESS certain words sparingly.

"Flaming" is an online term for messages that are highly emotional, angry or insulting. Be sure to check the tone of your message and keep your emotions in check.

Checklist

- Did you complete the to/from/subject information?
- Did you make your request or share your purpose in the first sentence or two?
- Did you keep the format and text plain and simple to avoid a garbled transmission?
- Did you write with clarity, effectiveness and courtesy?
- Did you check the content of your message for sensitivity, confidentiality and privacy issues?
- Did you include all the background information, project details or request specifics so the recipient understands your expectations?

E-Mail Pros and Cons	
Pros	*Cons*
Fast and easy delivery for "official" business	Questionable appropriateness
Tone can be very personal	Format often lost in recipient's copy
Can reach many readers at one time	Not completely secure and confidential
Users can print a clear hard copy	No "real" original hard copy with signature
Reader can save message in a file	Message must be very short
Easy for reader to reply	Recipient must have a computer and e-mail software
Inexpensive	
Can be forwarded to another reader	Can be forwarded accidentally
Eliminates unnecessary paper	
Allows off-site workers to collaborate on projects easily	

13

237

13

CHAPTER 14

Postcard Correspondence

Postcards are cost-effective correspondence tools that carry a lot of power. With the threat of mail-related terrorism, people are apprehensive about opening mail. Postcards can send a message, share information or promote an event easily, and yet avoid creating anxiety about a threat for the recipient.

This chapter has sample postcards you might choose to compose. The types of postcards included are:

- Seasonal Promotion
- Acknowledging a Customer for a Special Occasion
- Invitation
- Reminder

At the side of the page, you will find a brief explanation of each part of the postcard. The first example identifies each section of the message. Subsequent messages identify only changes to the basic format.

14

Step-by-Step Guide

Postcards are used as quick, informal forms of communication. They grab the recipient's attention, are easy to read and act on, and generally are more cost-effective than a formal letter with envelope. The ideal postcard is visually appealing, with a direct, concise message.

Step 1: Plan the main purpose of your correspondence. Keep it brief and to the point.

Step 2: Use catchy phrasing or specialized text to draw and keep the reader's attention. Write with clarity and creativity.

Step 3: Remember that a postcard can be viewed by anyone at any time. It is inappropriate to use this medium of communication to announce or share sensitive or confidential information.

Note: At the end of this chapter is a checklist to use when you write a postcard.

14

Seasonal Promotion

This postcard is used by a business to inform customers of a special promotion.

Capture the Spirit of Christmas!

Join us Saturday, December 2, for an afternoon of warmth and glad tidings as we welcome artist Gloria Patrick!

Gloria will be showcasing the latest addition to her sculpture series. "Angels Bending Near the Earth" is a breathtaking piece! Be sure to see it and visit with the artist about her work!

December 2 from 1:00 to 4:00
The Marketplace
1445 Broadway, Minneapolis, MN 42535

Announcement of Event

Confirmation of Date, Time and Place

Business Location Information

14

Acknowledging a Customer for a Special Occasion

This postcard acknowledges a customer's birthday with a special discount.

It's Your Birthday! Let us help you celebrate! Present this card and we will give you 15% off your purchase as our special gift to you! (Sale merchandise not included.) Valid for 60 days. *Happy Birthday!* from **Gracie's Gifts and Collectibles** 2891 Clairmont • Jacksonville, Florida 35695 (904) 555-6301	*Occasion* *Special Offer* *Business Logo*

14

Invitation

This business is using a postcard to invite customers to an open house.

You're Invited!

The Toulles House is having an Open House.
Please join us for caroling, cocoa and cookies
on Sunday, November 30,
anytime between 2:00 and 5:00 o'clock in the afternoon.

Toulles House
1601 Lexington Drive
Nantucket Sound, Massachusetts 21807
508.555.0202

Invitation

Event Information

14

Reminder

A postcard can be a very effective way of providing a quick, informal reminder.

Just a Reminder!

Your special order is ready for pickup!
Please call to make an appointment.

**Harvey's
Books and Papers**

10 Lindlewood Lane • Campaign, Washington 98940
509.555.0088

Reminder Information Request

14

Checklist

- Did you make your message brief and to the point?
- Did you use format and text that will catch the recipient's attention?
- Did you write with clarity and creativity?
- Did you check the content of your message for sensitivity, confidentiality and privacy issues?
- Did you include the background information, event description, location and contact information so the recipient understands the purpose of your message?

14

14

APPENDIX

Each example lists the following information in the format shown:

Addressee

> Form of Address

> *Salutation*

The eight broad categories of address are:

- Professional Ranks and Titles
- Federal, State and Local Government Officials
- Military Ranks
- Military Abbreviations
- Diplomats
- British Nobility
- Clerical and Religious Orders
- College and University Officials

Professional Ranks and Titles

Attorney

Mr. R. Allan Whiteman, Attorney-at-Law

or R. Allan Whiteman, Esq.

> *Dear Mr. Whiteman*
>
> *or Dear R. Allan Whiteman, Esq.*

Dentist

Jacqueline Lyster, D.D.S. (Office Address) or

Dr. Jacqueline Lyster (Home Address)

> *Dear Dr. Lyster*

Physician

Terry Thomlinson, M.D. (Office Address) or

Dr. Terry Thomlinson (Home Address)

> *Dear Dr. Thomlinson*

Veterinarian

Cathy Hines, D.V.M. (Office Address) or

Dr. Cathy Hines

> *Dear Dr. Hines*

Federal, State and Local Government Officials

Alderman

The Honorable Harriett Monson

Dear Ms. Monson

Assemblyman

See Representative, State

Associate Justice, Supreme Court

Mr. Justice Riley

The Supreme Court of the United States

Dear Mr. Justice

Cabinet Officers

Secretary of State

The Honorable Emily Williamson

The Secretary of State

Dear Madam Secretary

Attorney General

The Honorable Martin Trymore

Attorney General of the United States

Dear Sir

Chief Justice, Supreme Court

The Chief Justice of the United States

Dear Mr. Chief Justice

Commissioner

The Honorable C. Thomas Black

Dear Mr. Black

Former U.S. President

The Honorable Wilson Edwards

Dear Mr. Edwards

Governor

The Honorable Mary Simpson

Governor of Utah

Dear Governor Simpson

Judge, Federal

The Honorable Tomas Gonzales

United States District Judge

Dear Judge Gonzales

Judge, State or Local

Chief Judge of the Court of Appeals

The Honorable Larry Nelson

Dear Judge Nelson

Lieutenant Governor

The Honorable Aaron Gudenkauf

Lieutenant Governor of New Jersey

Dear Mr. Gudenkauf

Mayor

The Honorable W.M. Tied

Mayor of Greenville

Dear Mayor Tied

President, U.S.

The President

Dear Mr. President

Representative, State (same format for assemblyman)

The Honorable Amanda Brown

House of Representatives

State Capitol

Dear Ms. Brown

Representative, U.S.

The Honorable Blake Grahame

The United States House of Representatives

Dear Mr. Grahame

Senator, State

The Honorable Matthew K. Billings

The State Senate

State Capitol

Dear Senator Billings

Senator, U.S.

The Honorable Lillian Vries

United States Senate

Dear Senator Vries

Speaker, U.S. House of Representatives

The Honorable James B. Castle

Speaker of the House of Representatives

Dear Mr. Speaker

Vice President, U.S.

The Vice President

Executive Office Building

Dear Mr. Vice President

Military Ranks

Admiral, Vice Admiral, Rear Admiral

(Full Rank + Full Name + Comma + Abbreviation of Branch of Service)

Dear Admiral Rhodes

Airman

(Full Rank + Full Name + Comma + Abbreviation of Branch of Service)

Dear Airman Smith

Cadet

Cadet Jack Roberts

United States Military Academy

Dear Cadet Roberts

Captain (Air Force, Army, Coast Guard, Marine Corps or Navy)

(Full Rank + Full Name + Comma + Abbreviation of Branch of Service)

Dear Captain Lane

Colonel, Lieutenant Colonel (Air Force, Army or Marine Corps)

(Full Rank + Full Name + Comma + Abbreviation of Branch of Service)

Dear Colonel Arnold

Commander (Coast Guard or Navy)

(Full Rank + Full Name + Comma + Abbreviation of Branch of Service)

Dear Commander Grove

Corporal

(Full Rank + Full Name + Comma + Abbreviation of Branch of Service)

Dear Corporal Jones

First Lieutenant, Second Lieutenant (Air Force, Army or Marine Corps)

(Full Rank + Full Name + Comma + Abbreviation of Branch of Service)

Dear Lieutenant O'Shannon

General, Lieutenant General, Major General, Brigadier General (Air Force, Army or Marine Corps)

(Full Rank + Full Name + Comma + Abbreviation of Branch of Service)

Dear General Tubbs

Lieutenant Commander, Lieutenant, Lieutenant (JG), Ensign (Coast Guard, Navy)

(Full Rank + Full Name + Comma + Abbreviation of Branch of Service)

Dear Lieutenant Crites

Major (Air Force, Army or Marine Corps)

(Full Rank + Full Name + Comma + Abbreviation of Branch of Service)

Dear Major Giles

Master Sergeant (an example of other enlisted ranks having compound titles not shown here)

(Full Rank + Full Name + Comma + Abbreviation of Branch of Service)

Dear Sergeant Kaye

Midshipman

Midshipman Sally Cole

United States Naval Academy

Dear Midshipman Cole

Petty Officer and Chief Petty Officer

(Full Rank + Full Name + Comma + Abbreviation of Branch of Service)

Dear Mr. Schmidt

Dear Mr. Trank or

Dear Chief Trank

Private

(Full Rank + Full Name + Comma + Abbreviation of Branch of Service)

Dear Private Hesse

Seaman

(Full Rank + Full Name + Comma + Abbreviation of Branch of Service)

Dear Seaman Waters

Specialist

(Full Rank + Full Name + Comma + Abbreviation of Branch of Service)

Dear Mr. Ledford

Dear Ms. Fetters

Other Ranks Not Listed

(Full Rank + Full Name + Comma + Abbreviation of Branch of Service)

Military Abbreviations

Army	USA
Air Force	USAF
Marine	USM
Navy	USN

Diplomats

Ambassador to the U.S.

His Excellency Reginald Butters

The Ambassador of Bermuda

Excellency or

Dear Mr. Ambassador

American Ambassador

The Honorable J. Ellen Standford

Ambassador of the United States

Dear Ms. Ambassador or

Dear Madam Ambassador

American Charge d'Affaires

Allen White, Esq.

American Charge d'Affaires

Dear Sir

Minister to the U.S.

The Honorable Harry Lindermann

Minister of Liechtenstein

Dear Mr. Minister

Secretary-General, U.N.

Her Excellency Nbutu Montabi

Secretary-General of the United Nations

Dear Madam Secretary-General

British Nobility

The correct form is to address a representative of the royal person: "The Private Secretary to Her Majesty, the Queen."

Baron

The Right Honorable Lord Swarthmore

Dear Lord Swarthmore or

My Lord Swarthmore

Baroness

The Right Honorable Lady Swarthmore

Dear Lady Swarthmore or

My Lady Swarthmore

Duke

His Grace, The Duke of Marlington

Dear Duke of Marlington or

My Lord Duke

Duchess

Her Grace, The Duchess of Marlington

Dear Duchess or

My Lord Madam

Duke's Younger Son

The Lord William Wymore

Dear Lord William

Wife of Duke's Younger Son

The Lady William Wymore

Dear Lady William

Duke's Daughter

The Lady Regina Wymore

Dear Lady Regina

Earl

The Right Honorable the Earl of Tropingham

Dear Lord Cresswell or

My Lord Cresswell

Earl's Wife

The Right Honorable the Countess of Tropingham

Dear Lady Cresswell or

Madam Cresswell

Knight

Sir Reginald Williams

Dear Sir or

Dear Sir Reginald

Marquess

The Most Honorable the Marquess of Cullertshire

Dear Lord Ranson or

My Lord Ranson

Marchioness

The Most Honorable the Marchioness of Cullertshire

Dear Lady Ranson or

My Lady Ranson

Viscount

The Right Honorable the Viscount Lindsay

Dear Lord Lindsay or

My Lord Lindsay

Viscountess

The Right Honorable the Viscountess Lindsay

Dear Lady Lindsay or

My Lady Lindsay

Clerical and Religious Orders

Abbot

The Right Reverend Walter Jones, O.S.B.

Right Reverend and Abbot of St. Benedict's

Dear Father

Archbishop

The Most Reverend Archbishop Terrance Smith

Archbishop of Canada

Your Excellency or

Dear Archbishop

Archbishop, Anglican

To His Grace the Lord Archbishop of Canterbury

Your Grace or

My Dear Archbishop

Archdeacon

The Venerable the Archdeacon of New York

Venerable Sir

Bishop, Catholic

The Most Reverend Andrew Duncan

Bishop of New York

Your Excellency or

Dear Bishop Duncan

Bishop, Episcopal

The Right Reverend Samuel Thomas

Bishop of South Carolina

Dear Bishop Thomas

Bishop, Other Denominations

The Reverend Sandra Wright

Reverend Madam or

Dear Bishop Wright

Brotherhood, Catholic, Member of

Brother Williams, S.J.

Dear Brother James

Brotherhood, Catholic, Superior of

Brother Edward, S.J., Superior

Dear Brother Edward

Canon

The Reverend Dwight Boyd

Dear Canon Boyd

Cardinal

His Eminence, Harold Cardinal Lyte

Your Eminence or

Dear Cardinal Lyte

Clergyman, Protestant

The Reverend Catherine Wilson

Dear Madam or

Dear Ms. Wilson

(or, if having a doctorate degree)

The Reverend Dr. John Wong

Dear Dr. Wong

Dean (of a Cathedral)

The Very Reverend Calvin Schmidt

Very Reverend Sir

Dean Calvin Schmidt

Dear Dean Schmidt

Monsignor

The Right Reverend Monsignor Ellis

Dear Monsignor Ellis or

Right Reverend Monsignor

Patriarch (of an Eastern Church)

His Beatitude the Patriarch of New York

Most Reverend Lord

Pope

His Holiness, Pope John Paul II or

His Holiness, the Pope

Your Holiness or

Most Holy Father

Priest, Roman Catholic

The Reverend Lynn Martin

Dear Father Martin or

Reverend Father

Priest, Episcopal or Anglican

The Reverend Edward Arnold

Dear Mr. Arnold or

Dear Father Arnold

Priest, Denominational Protestant

The Reverend Cheryl Tims

Dear Ms. Tims

Rabbi

Rabbi Eli Gossman

Dear Rabbi Gossman

(if having a doctorate degree)

Rabbi David Weiss, D.D.

Dear Dr. Weiss

Sisterhood, Member of

Sister Mary Theresa, S

Dear Sister Mary Theresa or

Dear Sister

Sisterhood, Superior of

The Reverend Mother Superior, S

Reverend Mother

College and University Officials

Dean of a College or University

Dean Mary Carlson

Dear Dean Carlson

President of a College or University

President James Bagg

Dear President Bagg

Professor of a College or University

Professor Linda Tripp

Dear Professor Tripp

Note: The college official's educational degrees, if known, may be added after the name.

*I*NDEX

    letter to legislator showing concern   105
    letter to legislator showing support   104
    membership invitation   96
    refusal of a request   97
    solicitation of funds   87–88
    thank you   93
completeness   6-7
compliment letter   101
compliment to employee for work   236
complimentary close   12
concise   6
concrete terms   7
condolence letters   123-133
    brother   131
    business associate   125
    child   130
    father   127
    husband   129
    mother   126
    sister   132
    wife   128
confidential   10
confirmation to speaker   184
confirming sales order   47–48
congratulations   71–73, 109, 110
considerations of a business letter   2-3
    audience   2
    purpose   3
    style/organization   3
    subject   2
constructive writing   7
conversational style   6
correct writing   7
correcting an error   199
correction, asking for a   225
cover letter for resumé   145–146
customer relations letters   191-212
    acknowledging a complaint   194
        disclaiming responsibility   197
        explaining a misunderstanding   198
    acknowledging an order
        back order   201
        explaining shipment procedures   202
    apologizing for an employee's action   203
    correcting an error   199
    following up on a complaint   195
    general apology   200
    general appreciation   193

YOUR BACK-OF-THE-BOOK STORE

ORDER FORM

Because you already know the value of National Press Publications Desktop Handbooks and Business User's Manuals, here's a time-saving way to purchase more career-building resources from our convenient bookstore.

- IT'S EASY … Just make your selections, then visit us on the Web, mail, call or fax your order. (See back for details.)
- INCREASE YOUR EFFECTIVENESS … Books in these two series have sold more than two million copies and are known as reliable sources of instantly helpful information.
- THEY'RE CONVENIENT TO USE … Each handbook is durable, concise and filled with quality advice that will last you all the way to the boardroom.

60-MINUTE TRAINING SERIES™ HANDBOOKS

TITLE	ITEM #	RETAIL PRICE*	QTY.	TOTAL
8 Steps for Highly Effective Negotiations	#424	$14.95		
Assertiveness	#4422	$14.95		
Balancing Career and Family	#4152	$14.95		
Common Ground	#4122	$14.95		
The Essentials of Business Writing	#4310	$14.95		
Everyday Parenting Solutions	#4862	$14.95		
Exceptional Customer Service	#4882	$14.95		
Fear & Anger: Control Your Emotions	#4302	$14.95		
Fundamentals of Planning	#4301	$14.95		
Getting Things Done	#4112	$14.95		
How to Coach an Effective Team	#4308	$14.95		
How to De-Junk Your Life	#4306	$14.95		
How to Handle Conflict and Confrontation	#4952	$14.95		
How to Manage Your Boss	#493	$14.95		
How to Supervise People	#4102	$14.95		
How to Work With People	#4032	$14.95		
Inspire and Motivate: Performance Reviews	#4232	$14.95		
Listen Up: Hear What's Really Being Said	#4172	$14.95		
Motivation and Goal-Setting	#4962	$14.95		
A New Attitude	#4432	$14.95		
The New Dynamic Comm. Skills for Women	#4309	$14.95		
The Polished Professional	#4262	$14.95		
The Power of Innovative Thinking	#428	$14.95		
The Power of Self-Managed Teams	#4222	$14.95		
Powerful Communication Skills	#4132	$14.95		
Present With Confidence	#4612	$14.95		
The Secret to Developing Peak Performers	#4962	$14.95		
Self-Esteem: The Power to Be Your Best	#4642	$14.95		
Shortcuts to Organized Files and Records	#4307	$14.95		
The Stress Management Handbook	#4842	$14.95		
Supreme Teams: How to Make Teams Work	#4303	$14.95		
Thriving on Change	#4212	$14.95		
Women and Leadership	#4632	$14.95		

Business User's Manuals — Self-Study, Interactive Guides

TITLE	RETAIL PRICE	QTY.	TOTAL
The Assertive Advantage #439	$26.95		
Being OK Just Isn't Enough #5407	$26.95		
Business Letters for Busy People #449	$26.95		
Dealing With Conflict and Anger #5402	$26.95		
Complete Guide to Finding and Hiring the Right People #54052	$26.95		
High-Impact Presentation and Training Skills #4382	$26.95		
Learn to Listen #446	$26.95		
The Manager's Role as Coach #456	$26.95		
The Memory System #452	$26.95		
Negaholics® No More #5406	$26.95		
Parenting the Other Chick's Eggs #5404	$26.95		
Taking AIM On Leadership #5401	$26.95		
Prioritize, Organize: Art of Getting It Done 2nd ed. #4532	$26.95		
The Promotable Woman #450	$26.95		
Think Like a Manager 3rd ed. #4513	$26.95		
Working Woman's Comm. Survival Guide #5172	$29.95		

SPECIAL OFFER:
Orders over $150.00 receive
FREE SHIPPING

Prices and availability subject to change without notice.

Subtotal	$
Add 7% Sales Tax *(Or add appropriate state and local tax)*	$
Shipping and Handling *($6 one item; 50¢ each additional item)*	$
Total	$

VOLUME DISCOUNTS AVAILABLE — CALL 1-800-258-7248

Name_____Title_____

Organization _____

Address _____

City _____State/Province _____ZIP/Postal Code _____

Payment choices:
❑ Enclosed is my check/money order payable to National Seminars.
❑ Please charge to: ❑ MasterCard   ❑ VISA   ❑ American Express

Signature _____Exp. Date _____Card Number _____
❑ Purchase Order #_____

MAIL: Complete and mail order form
with payment to:
**National Press Publications
P.O. Box 419107
Kansas City, MO 64141-6107**

PHONE:
Call toll-free **1-800-258-7248**

FAX:
1-913-432-0824

INTERNET: www.NationalSeminarsTraining.com